The Literature of Theology:
A Guide for Students and Pastors

The Literature
of Theology:
A Guide for Students
and Pastors

John A. Bollier

The Westminster Press
Philadelphia

First edition

Published by The Westminster Press®

Philadelphia, Pennsylvania

PRINTED IN THE UNITED STATES OF AMERICA

9 8 7 6 5 4 3 2 1

Library of Congress Cataloging in Publication Data

Bollier, John A   1927–
    The literature of theology.

    Includes index.
    1. Theology—Bibliography. I. Title.
Z7751.B67 [BR118]   016.23   78-10962
ISBN 0-664-24225-1

To Trudy
Proverbs 31:10

Contents

Contents

Preface

This work is intended for the theological student, both Protestant and Catholic, for the parish minister or priest, as well as for the layperson who is seeking an introduction to the vast and often overwhelming body of theological literature. The librarian who may not be trained in theology, but who is required to provide reference service or do book selection in the area of theology, will also find this a useful manual.

The purpose of this work is to help the reader become independent in finding the books, the journal articles, or the information needed in the pursuit of either academic study or professional ministry. It lists and annotates over 540 reference tools, such as bibliographies, encyclopedias, dictionaries, indexes, abstracts, handbooks, guides, manuals, catalogs, and commentaries, all of which provide the information or literature citations for any subject required. There are also extensive sections on English-language Bible versions and translations.

As a rule, this work does not list monographs, which are intended to be read from cover to cover, but rather only reference works, which are opened at a particular page and consulted either for specific information or for further bibliography of monographic or journal literature. The few monographs that are listed are included because of the extensive "hidden" bibliographies they contain.

The number of titles published each year in the United States and Great Britain alone is now in the neighborhood of 120,000. (*The Bowker Annual of Library and Book Trade Information,* 22d ed. [New York and London: R. R. Bowker Company, 1977], p. 452.) Journal articles, reports and proceedings of learned societies, and other serial literature likewise have reached overwhelming proportions. Faced with such a sea of material, the reader may have one of two predictable reactions: the first is to throw up one's hands in despair, succumb to the flood, and read only what happens to come across one's desk; the second is to become a specialist in a narrow field and make a valiant effort to keep up with one's field and disregard everything else. This work attempts to show a third and "more excellent way" for the theological student, the parish pastor, the layperson, or the librarian, all of whom must be generalists in this age of increasing specialization. By mastering the tools described in this work, one is able to gain what librarians call "bibliographic control" of the literature on any topic. With such a skill, the pastor can make his or her own reading list of relevant material without being dependent on the personal recommendation of the professor, who is usually no longer near at hand as in student days. And with this same skill, the student can save hours, days, or even weeks of undirected and fruitless search for materials required for term papers or research projects.

This work grew out of a course on Theological Bibliography and Research Methodology that I developed at Yale Divinity School with the help of a grant from the Association of Theological Schools in the United States and Canada. Because I served as a pastor for eighteen years and have worked as a theological librarian for the past seven years, I am intimately acquainted with the informational needs of the pastor as well as the rich bibliographic and reference resources that are available for meeting those needs. As most theological seminaries have not seriously addressed themselves to their students' lack of sophisticated bibliographic skills, I have tried to bring my knowledge and experience in librarianship to the service of the ministry. The present book is the result of this effort.

This is obviously a selective and not an exhaustive bibliography. Others certainly would have made different choices of materials to be included. However, I have chosen those works which I believe are most useful to the theological student and the parish pastor. Consequently, there are very few foreign-language works included. For those who are engaged in advanced research and require such tools, of which there is a wealth, especially in German, I would recommend Gerhard Schwinge, *Bibliographische Nachschlagewerke zur Theologie und ihren Grenzgebieten* (no. 19).

Generally emphasis has been placed on more recent works. But if a work is still useful and has not been superseded, it is included regardless of its imprint date. In most of the areas I have covered it would be possible to go into more depth, but if I did so, the reader who is seeking an introduction to theological literature would again begin to groan in despair. I have instead attempted to select enough basic tools in each field so that the reader with a mastery of these may proceed to whatever depth or breadth may be required. The beauty of reference and bibliographic tools is that they always point beyond themselves to more expansive horizons.

Some sections, such as those on the Bible, church history, and the Catholic Church are considerably longer than others, such as the sections on systematic theology, practical theology, or particular Protestant denominations. This is not due to any theological or bibliographic bias on my part, but simply reflects the fact that some subjects have richer bibliographic resources than others. I would hope that aspiring young scholars, noting the paucity of reference and bibliographic tools in some fields, may discover new challenges for the employment of their subject expertise in helping to fill these lacunae.

While there is a chapter dealing specifically with Protestant, Catholic, and Jewish works, such neat divisions are no longer always relevant in the theological enterprise today. Consequently, the tools listed and described throughout this work are of value and of use to all those included within the broad spectrum of the Judeo-Christian tradition. A few tools for Eastern religions are included, but no attempt has been made to provide any depth in these areas. As the literature for such study is so vast and varied, I would recommend that those who seek a bibliographic introduction to these religions begin with Charles J. Adams, ed., *A Reader's Guide to the Great Religions* (no. 495).

Arranging so many varied works as here listed of necessity requires certain arbitrary decisions. However, I have generally followed the divisions of the classical theological curriculum: Biblical studies, systematic theology, historical studies, and practical theology. Where a work could equally well appear in two places, I have listed it in only one place and made a cross-reference at the other.

I have not drawn any hard-and-fast line between theological works on the one hand and "general" or "secular" works on the other. Not only is this not considered good theology; it is not good bibliography either. The general works, such as the *National Union Catalog, Pre-1956 Imprints* (no. 30) or the *Union List of Serials in Libraries in the United States and Canada* (no. 67), cast a broad net that catches both theological and nontheological works alike.

Moreover, within any given section I have followed whatever arrangement I felt would be most useful to the reader. Thus, works may be listed alphabetically by author, or chronologically, or in reverse chronological order from more recent to older, or in classified, logical order. A detailed table of contents and an author and title index are provided to help the reader locate entries quickly and easily.

Brief descriptive rather than critical evaluations are provided for virtually all entries. These more objective statements concerning the contents, purpose, scope, arrangement, depth, and perspective of each work should provide the reader with sufficient data to determine whether it is worthwhile to retrieve a particular work for the informational or bibliographic needs at hand.

To the reader who is not initiated into the mysteries of librarianship, the choice of whether certain entries begin with the author's/editor's name or with the title of the work may seem arbitrary. However, one informed of these secrets knows that while certain forms and procedures in librarianship may be optional, nothing is arbitrary. The *Anglo-American Cataloging Rules,* prepared by the American Library Association, the Library of Congress, the Library Association, and the Canadian Library Association (Chicago: American Library Association, 1967), set the standards by which the faithful abide and ever seek to bring order out of chaos. These *Rules* have guided the form of entry followed in this book. This corresponds to the form of entry used in most library catalogs, and will facilitate access to such catalogs.

Many more people have aided me in this work than I can possibly acknowledge here. However, I would like to express my gratitude to the following important contributors: my students at Yale Divinity School, who by their receptiveness demonstrated the need for this type of manual; Stephen L. Peterson, Yale Divinity School Librarian, and my other colleagues on the Yale Divinity School Library staff, who encouraged me in this task and covered for me when I neglected my other duties to complete it; the Yale Divinity School faculty, which permitted me to engage in bibliographic instruction; Rutherford D. Rogers, Yale University Librarian, and Donald B. Engley, Associate University Librarian, who made possible a research leave for completing the manuscript; the Association of Theological Schools in the United States and Canada for the initial grant to develop the course in bibliographic instruction out of which this work arose; Marilyn Paarlberg, who served as the research assistant and typist for the preliminary edition used by my class for three years; Nona Jenkins, who typed this manuscript; Richard Duffield, who helped prepare the index; and my wife, Trudy, for her unfailing support in this and all the other tasks I have undertaken in my ministry.

JOHN A. BOLLIER

Yale Divinity School Library
New Haven, Connecticut

CHAPTER I

Bibliography

GUIDES AND MANUALS

COMPREHENSIVE GUIDES AND MANUALS

A guide or manual is a reference tool that provides an overview of the important literature of an academic discipline. Unfortunately, theology, with its voluminous current and retrospective literature, does not have an abundance of such tools. Helping to offset this lack, however, are two comprehensive guides, each of which has a considerable section devoted to Religion. Both works are available in almost every academic and public library.

1. Sheehy, Eugene P. *Guide to Reference Books.* 9th ed. Chicago: American Library Association, 1976. 1,015 pp.

Covers general reference works, the humanities, social sciences, history and area studies, pure and applied sciences. Thorough coverage, brief annotations; international in scope, with emphasis on American works. A source well known to librarians, and one that could profitably be used by students and scholars. Religion section, pp. 252–283.

2. Walford, Albert John, ed. *Guide to Reference Materials.* 2d ed. London: The Library Association, 1966–1970. 3 vols.

Contents: Vol. 1, Science and technology; Vol. 2, Philosophy and psychology, religion, social sciences, geography, biography, and history; Vol. 3, Generalities, languages, the arts, and literature. Arranged according to the Universal Decimal Classification system; annotates works listed and often cites bibliographies "hidden" in nonreference books; emphasis on British publications. Religion section, Vol. 2, pp. 22–61.

RECENT PROTESTANT GUIDES AND MANUALS

A number of seminary faculties produce guides from time to time for their students and alumni/ae in parish ministry. Among such works listed in order from the most recent are the following:

3. Richmond, Va. Union Theological Seminary. *Essential Books for a Pastor's Library: Basic and Recommended Works.* 4th ed. Richmond, Va.: Union Theological Seminary, 1968. 119 pp.

Provides brief annotations for works in areas of general reference, Bible, history and philosophy of history, church history, doctrinal theology, ethics, ministry.

4. Andover Newton Theological School, Newton Centre, Mass. *Theological Bibliographies; Essential Books for a Minister's Library.* Published as the Sept. 1963 issue of *Andover Newton Quarterly* (New Series, Vol. 4, No. 1). 138 pp.

Classified arrangement. Selected and annotated by members of the faculty.

5. New York (City). Union Theological Seminary. *A Basic Bibliography for Ministers.* 2d ed. New York: Union Theological Seminary, 1960. 139 pp.

Classified arrangement. Selection and annotation by 27 members of the faculty.

Other recent Protestant guides produced by an individual author or compiler include the following in order from the most recent:

6. Barber, Cyril J. *The Minister's Library.* Grand Rapids, Mich.: Baker Book House, 1974. 378 pp.

Classified arrangement with brief annotations. "Books espousing a theological viewpoint which is not in keeping with a conservative evangelical position have been identified with a dagger" (p. 39). Emphasis is on exposition. "Books on pastoral theology, homiletics, counseling, philosophy of religion, and historical theology, while not ignored, are subordinated to the primary purpose of the work" (Introduction).

7. Kennedy, James R., Jr. *Library Research Guide for Reli-*

gion and Theology; Illustrated Search Strategy and Sources. Ann
Arbor, Mich.: Pierian Press, 1973. 53 pp. (Library Research
Guide series, No. 1.)

A useful tool for learning to do library research. Greater
emphasis on search strategy than discussion of theological literature. An appendix, pp. 43–51, lists in classified order about 250
theological reference tools.

8. Sayre, John L., and Hamburger, Roberta. *Tools for Theological Research.* 5th ed. Enid, Okla.: Seminary Press, 1978. 90
pp.

Classified, annotated, with author-title index. Part I includes
the 103 reference tools given primary emphasis in the Theological Bibliography course at the Phillips University Graduate
Seminary. Part II includes supplementary tools that are useful
when doing extensive research.

9. Aldrich, Ella V., and Camp, Thomas Edward. *Using Theological Books and Libraries.* Englewood Cliffs, N.J.: Prentice-
Hall, Inc., 1963. 119 pp.

Lists and annotates some 500 general and theological reference tools, such as periodical indexes, abstracts, bibliographies,
dictionaries, encyclopedias. While now somewhat out of date, it
still provides much useful information for theological students.

10. Montgomery, John Warwick. *The Writing of Research
Papers in Theology; An Introductory Lecture.* Chicago: University of Chicago Divinity School, 1959. 38 pp.

Lists 150 basic reference tools, pp. 22–36, some of which are
discussed in the lecture.

NINETEENTH-CENTURY PROTESTANT GUIDES
AND MANUALS

In the nineteenth century, German, British, and American
theologians made serious scholarly efforts to write detailed
guides to the literature of theology. While now outdated, these
works still are useful for a historical study of the various areas
of theology. Included in these works are:

11. Cave, Alfred. *An Introduction to Theology; Its Principles,
Its Branches, Its Results, and Its Literature.* 2d ed. Edinburgh:
T. & T. Clark, 1896. 610 pp.

After each section there are one or two books listed as "Introductory" to the topic followed by a much longer list of books in English, German, and French: "For more advanced study." The section on "Biblical Theology," pp. 240–423, far exceeds all others in breadth and coverage. The author states, "At the moment this inequality is unavoidable; so much more is known of the Bible than any other branch of theology." Although it is over eighty years since this statement was made, it is still true that Biblical studies have the most extensive and in-depth bibliographic coverage of all the theological disciplines.

12. Darling, James. *Cyclopaedia Bibliographica: A Library Manual of Theological and General Literature, and Guide to Books for Authors, Preachers, Students, and Literary Men.* London: James Darling, 1854–1859. 2 vols.

A massive, detailed, scholarly work, Vol. 1 lists works alphabetically by author, often gives brief biographical information and occasional annotations. Vol. 2, entitled "Subjects, Holy Scriptures," lists works on the Bible in classified order; with a subject index.

13. Hagenbach, Karl Rudolf. *Theological Encyclopaedia and Methodology; on the basis of Hagenbach.* Translated and enlarged by George R. Crooks and John F. Hurst. New York: Phillips and Hunt, 1884. 596 pp.

A translation of the German work with a bibliography greatly enlarged "by adding the titles of English and American books in each department" (Preface).

14. Hurst, John Fletcher. *The Literature of Theology; A Classified Bibliography of Theological and General Religious Literature.* New York: Hunt and Eaton; Cincinnati: Cranston and Curts, 1896. 757 pp.

A comprehensive bibliography of "the best and most desirable books in Theology and General Religious Literature published in Great Britain, the United States, and the Dominion of Canada" (Preface). Hurst, a Methodist bishop and scholar, who served as president of Drew and chancellor of American University, compiled an earlier bibliography, *Bibliotheca Theologica* (New York: Charles Scribner's Sons, 1883), which is superseded by the work cited here.

15. Schaff, Philip. *Theological Propaedeutic; A General Intro-*

duction to the Study of Theology, Exegetical, Historical, Systematic, and Practical Including Encyclopaedia, Methodology and Bibliography. 4th ed. New York: Charles Scribner's Sons, 1898. (copr. 1893.) 596 pp.

Introductory and bibliographic materials are interspersed throughout this impressive work written by the outstanding American church historian and theologian. This is the first such original work written for American students. Schaff writes: "Propaedeutic is as yet a new study in this country, but it should be taught in every theological institution. No course is more necessary and useful for beginners" (Preface). A bibliography entitled "A ministerial library" compiled by Samuel Macauley Jackson and arranged in the order of the *Propaedeutic* is appended, pp. 539–596.

RECENT CATHOLIC GUIDES AND MANUALS

16. Mitros, Joseph F. *Religions, A Select, Classified Bibliography.* New York: Learned Publications, 1973. 435 pp. (Philosophical Questions Series, No. 8.)

The section on Christianity is over 200 pages, twice the length of the bibliographies for all the other religions of the world. This section covers Christianity's "history, various denominations and aspects of life; a particular coverage is given to its beginnings in the form of Biblical and Patristic studies" (Introduction). The literature listed includes reference books, monographs, periodicals, primary and secondary sources. A detailed table of contents and an author index serve as useful finding guides.

17. McCabe, James Patrick. *Critical Guide to Catholic Reference Books.* Littleton, Colo.: Libraries Unlimited, Inc., 1971. 287 pp.

A scholarly, thorough work, listing over 900 Catholic reference tools with annotations and quotations from critical reviews in Catholic sources. Covers general works, theology, humanities, social sciences, history. Written as a University of Michigan Ph.D. dissertation. Includes author, title, subject index. No single Protestant-oriented work is comparable.

18. Steiner, Urban J. *Contemporary Theology, A Reading*

28 *The Literature of Theology*

Guide. Collegeville, Minn.: Liturgical Press, 1965. 111 pp.

Written for the Catholic priest and seminarian; mostly current, in-print works in classified order. Descriptive and occasionally evaluative annotations. Section on "Sacred Scripture" is the longest, but the author states: "In the spirit of the Second Vatican Council, we have attempted to give a new prominence to fields of liturgy, as well as ecumenism and pastoral theology" (Introduction). Author index and list of publishers and their addresses appended.

GERMAN AND FRENCH GUIDES AND MANUALS

For more advanced students who require the use of reference and bibliographic tools in languages besides English, the following two works should be consulted:

19. Schwinge, Gerhard. *Bibliographische Nachschlagewerke zur Theologie und ihren Grenzgebieten.* Munich: Verlag Dokumentation, 1975. 232 pp.

A comprehensive, annotated, classified bibliography of general, theological, and related reference works with author-title index and subject index. A basic tool to provide an introduction to the vast theological reference literature in German.

20. Malclès, Louise-Noëlle. *Les Sources du Travail Bibliographique.* Geneva: E. Droz; Lille: Giard, 1950–1958, 3 vols. in 4. (Reprinted 1965.)

"Sciences Religieuses" in Vol. 2, pp. 434–480. The standard comprehensive French reference guide, comparable to the American Sheehy (no. 1) and the British Walford (no. 2).

BIBLIOGRAPHY OF BIBLIOGRAPHIES

While its name may be confusing, this type of work can be most helpful for the researcher. Someone who has taken the time and effort to collect, arrange, and describe bibliographies can save the researcher countless hours of futile inquiry by taking him directly to the type of bibliography he is seeking. In addition to using the works listed below, one can also usually find bibliographies by turning to the library catalog and looking for the subheading "Bibliography" under any given subject heading.

21. Barrow, John Graves. *A Bibliography of Bibliographies in Religion.* Ann Arbor, Mich.: Edwards Brothers, Inc., 1955. 489 pp.

Based upon the author's 1930 Yale Ph.D. dissertation, this impressive work lists separately published bibliographies by subject and chronologically within subjects from the fifteenth century to the present. Brief annotations and locations in principal American and European libraries are given. Author-subject index included. Coverage is primarily for Christianity. Now old, but still not superseded.

22. Smith, Wilbur M. *A List of Bibliographies of Theological and Biblical Literature Published in Great Britain and America, 1595–1931; With Critical, Biographical and Bibliographical Notes.* Coatesville, Pa., 1931. 62 pp.

Just as this slender volume was about to go to the printer's, the author learned of Barrow's comprehensive dissertation (no. 21) which had just been completed. With Barrow's encouragement and offer of additional titles, Smith made the additions and proceeded to publish this informative little work. As the title suggests, its scope is limited to Biblical and theological studies. Church history, missions, religious education, and non-Christian religions are not included. Titles are arranged chronologically. Author index included. One should take note in this day of "busy" pastors and "active" churches that Smith produced this work while he was pastor of the First Presbyterian Church of Coatesville, Pa.

For a bibliography of New Testament bibliographies, see no. 245.

In addition to the special theologically oriented bibliographies of bibliography, the general, comprehensive works of this type often contain numerous entries in the area of theology or religion. The following are profitable to the theological student:

23. Besterman, Theodore. *A World Bibliography of Bibliographies and of Bibliographical Catalogues, Calendars, Abstracts, Digests, Indexes, and the Like.* 4th ed., rev. and greatly enl. Lausanne: Societas Bibliographica, 1965–1966. 5 vols.

Lists only separately published bibliographies; classified arrangement, alphabetical under subject; Vol. 5 is index to the whole work. "Theology" section is in Vol. 4, pp. 6074–6121.

This work has been reprinted in sections, which may be purchased separately. A unique work, especially since it is the product of a single compiler.

24. *Bibliographic Index; A Cumulative Bibliography of Bibliographies.* 1937 to date. New York: The H. W. Wilson Company, 1938 to date.

Published semiannually with an annual cumulation. Includes bibliographies published separately as well as those with fifty or more entries appearing as parts of books or periodicals. Examines about 2,200 periodicals in Western languages for bibliographic material. Arranged alphabetically by subject. Useful separately or as a complement to Besterman (no. 23).

25. Collison, Robert L. *Bibliographies, Subject and National; A Guide to Their Contents, Arrangement and Use.* 3d ed., rev. and enl. London: Crosby Lockwood, 1968. 203 pp.

Includes nearly 500 carefully selected and well-annotated bibliographies. Subject bibliographies in Part I are in classified order including "Theology and Religion," pp. 13–20. Part II includes universal bibliographies and national bibliographies of Great Britain, the United States, France, and Germany.

LIBRARY CATALOGS

The published catalogs of large research libraries are the most comprehensive form of bibliography today. No longer need one be in the particular library to have bibliographic access to its collection, since library catalogs are duplicated and published in book form and widely dispersed in academic and public libraries throughout the world. Listed below are the catalogs in book form of an outstanding American theological library and an outstanding British theological library. These are followed by the published catalogs of the comprehensive "national" libraries of the United States, Great Britain, and France.

26. New York (City). Union Theological Seminary. Library. *The Shelf List of the Union Theological Seminary Library in New York City; In Classification Order.* Boston: G. K. Hall & Company, 1960. 10 vols.

Lists some 203,000 titles in the order in which they are actually arranged on the shelf. Easy subject access may be had by using it in conjunction with the following work:

27. ————. *Classification of the Library of Union Theological Seminary in the City of New York.* Prepared by Julia Pettee. Rev. and enl. ed., with additions and corrections, 1939 to Dec. 1966, ed. by Ruth C. Eisenhart. New York: Union Theological Seminary, 1967. 793 pp.

Contains the detailed classification schedule of the Union Theological Seminary classification system. By finding the classification number of a particular subject, the researcher can then turn to that section of the shelf list catalog (no. 26) to discover this particular library's books on that subject. Includes a subject index.

28. ————. *Alphabetical Arrangement of Main Entries from the Shelf List.* Boston: G. K. Hall & Company, 1960 (i.e., 1965). 10 vols.

Contains essentially the same information as the shelf list catalog (no. 26). However, the 191,000 cards are arranged alphabetically by author.

29. Williams Library, London. *Catalogue of the Library in Red Cross Street, Cripplegate;* founded pursuant to the will of the Reverend Daniel Williams, D.D., who died in the year 1716. London: Printed and sold by R. and J. E. Taylor, 1841. 2 vols.

————. ————. Appendix. London: Printed by Woodfall and Kinder, 1854. 150 pp.

Williams Library, London. *Catalogue of Accessions, 1900–1950.* London: Dr. Williams Trust, 1955. 776 pp.

————. *Catalogue of Accessions,* Vol. 2, 1951–1960. London: Dr. Williams Trust, 1961. 181 pp.

————. *Catalogue of Accessions,* Vol. 3, 1961–1970. London: Dr. Williams Trust, 1972. 261 pp.

Begun in 1715 with some 10,000 volumes from the personal library of Dr. Daniel Williams (ca. 1643–1717), a prominent Presbyterian minister in Ireland and later London, along with that of Dr. William Bates, the collection has been continued by the Dr. Williams Trust and now includes over 100,000 volumes in theology, church history, philosophy, ethics, and non-Christian religions. The catalogs are arranged in alphabetical order by author and give brief details on place and date of publication. A useful supplement to each volume lists publications of British and foreign learned societies as well as a wide range of periodicals. The collection is especially strong in Nonconformist literature. For a separate catalog of this portion of the collection, see no. 359.

30. *National Union Catalog, Pre-1956 Imprints.* A cumulative author list representing Library of Congress printed cards and titles reported by other American libraries. London: Mansell Information/Publishing, Ltd., 1968–1978. Vols. 1–584. (In progress.)

Approximately five volumes per month are being published until the projected 610 volumes are completed. The volumes on "Bible" have been delayed because of their complexity. When completed, this momentous work will supersede all previously published Library of Congress main entry catalogs. For a history of these earlier catalogs, consult Sheehy (no. 1), pp. 9–11. The completed work will list some ten million works not only at the Library of Congress but in some 700 other research libraries in the United States and Canada that report their holdings to the Library of Congress. This tool is, thus, a basic finding guide to locating a particular work. As in the earlier editions, entries are listed by author only.

31. *National Union Catalog, 1956 Through 1967.* A cumulative author list representing Library of Congress printed cards and titles reported by other American libraries. Totowa, N.J.: Rowman and Littlefield, Inc., 1970–1972. 125 vols.

National Union Catalog: A cumulative author list representing Library of Congress printed cards and titles reported by other American libraries, 1968–1972. Ann Arbor: J. W. Edwards Publishers, Inc., 1973. 104 vols.

These works serve as continuations of the *National Union Catalog, Pre-1956 Imprints* (no. 30). For more current bibliographic or location information, consult the following:

National Union Catalog: A cumulative author list. Washington, D.C.: Library of Congress, Card Division. Monthly, with quarterly and annual cumulations.

32. *Library of Congress Catalog, Books: Subjects, 1950–1954.* A cumulative list of works represented by Library of Congress printed cards. Ann Arbor: J. W. Edwards, Inc., 1955. 20 vols.

———. ———. 1955–1959. Paterson, N.J.: Pageant Books, Inc., 1960. 22 vols.

———. ———. 1960–1964. Ann Arbor: J. W. Edwards, Inc., 1965. 25 vols.

———. ———. 1965–1969. Ann Arbor: J. W. Edwards, Inc., 1970. 42 vols.

Published quarterly with annual and five-year cumulations. A most useful subject approach to books printed since 1945 and cataloged by the Library of Congress or one of the libraries participating in its cooperative cataloging program within the periods covered. Subjects are arranged alphabetically and books within a subject are arranged alphabetically by author. Provides easy bibliographic access to the more recent theological literature on a subject basis. Should be used in conjunction with the following work:

33. U.S. Library of Congress. Subject Cataloging Division. *Library of Congress Subject Headings.* 8th ed. Washington, D.C.: Library of Congress, 1975. 2 vols.

Kept up to date by quarterly cumulative supplements. This is the thesaurus containing the exact form of the terminology used by the Library of Congress in its subject headings. These same subject headings are used in the listing of books in the *Library of Congress Catalog, Books: Subjects* (no. 32), and in the public catalogs of most libraries using the Library of Congress classification system. Sometimes library users fail to find books on a given subject because they are not looking under the right subject heading. This work serves as an index to a public catalog, giving the exact form of the subject headings used on Library of Congress catalog cards.

34. British Museum. Department of Printed Books. *General Catalogue of Printed Books.* Photolithographic edition to 1955. London: Trustees of the British Museum, 1959–1966. 263 vols.

———. ———. *Ten-year Supplement, 1956–1965.* London: Trustees of the British Museum, 1968. 50 vols.

———. ———. *Five-year Supplement, 1966–1970.* London: Trustees of the British Museum, 1971. 26 vols.

Primarily an author catalog of the most outstanding collection of British publications. Of special interest to theological students are the two volumes on "Bible" and the three volumes on "Liturgies."

35. Paris. Bibliothèque Nationale. *Catalogue Général des Livres Imprimés: Auteurs.* Paris: Imprimerie Nationale, 1900–1972. 215 vols.

After volume 189 no entries past 1959 are included. Such later works are included in the first five-year supplement:

————. ————. 1960–1964. Paris: Imprimerie Nationale, 1965–1967. 12 vols.

RETROSPECTIVE BIBLIOGRAPHY

Retrospective bibliography is usually published singly and irregularly and lists works that have appeared anytime in the past, whereas current bibliography appears at regular and frequent intervals and attempts to list works that have been published recently. Presented in this section are retrospective general theological bibliographies of the last two decades.

36. Morris, Raymond P. *A Theological Book List.* Produced by the Theological Education Fund of the International Missionary Council for the theological seminaries and colleges in Africa, Asia, Latin America, and the Southwest Pacific. Oxford: Basil Blackwell & Mott, Ltd.; Naperville, Ill.: Alec R. Allenson, Inc., 1960. 242 pp.

A listing of 5,472 works, primarily in English, for aiding development of theological libraries in Third World countries. Because of its detailed classified arrangement, it is a most useful tool as a starting point for the student in developing subject bibliography in most areas of theology or religion. Includes author index. Continued by the following:

37. The Theological Education Fund, a service of the Commission on World Mission and Evangelism of the World Council of Churches, for theological seminaries and colleges in Africa, Asia, Latin America, and the Southwest Pacific. *A Theological Book List.* Oxford: Basil Blackwell & Mott, Ltd.; Naperville, Ill.: Alec R. Allenson, Inc., 1963. Various pagings.

Includes separate sections on works in English, French, German, Portuguese, and Spanish.

38. ————. *A Theological Book List 1968.* London: World

Council of Churches, 1968. 121 pp.

Includes sections on works in English, French, Portuguese, and Spanish. No German section included because of "the availability of comprehensive catalogues of theological books in German, notably, *Das Evangelische Schriftum* published periodically by the Vereinigung Evangelischer Buchhändler e.V., Stuttgart" (Preface). Contains titles produced 1963–1966. "Unlike its predecessors the English section includes introductory articles surveying the more significant publications in particular disciplines since 1960" (Preface).

39. American Theological Library Association. *Aids to a Theological Library; Selected Basic Reference Books and Periodicals.* Published by the American Theological Library Association Library Development Program for the American Association of Theological Schools. Rev., 1969. 95 pp.

Lists basic theological bibliographic and reference tools in classified order without annotation. Includes a name index and an extensive list of "scholarly periodicals currently published and useful for theological education." Intended for library acquisition purposes, but useful to students for identifying basic tools for developing subject bibliography. Updated by the following:

40. Trotti, John B., ed. *Aids to a Theological Library.* Missoula, Mont.: Scholars Press for the American Theological Library Association, 1977. (Library Aids, No. 1). 69 pp.

Classified order, but without index, table of contents, or annotations.

41. O'Brien, Elmer, ed. *Theology in Transition; A Bibliographic Evaluation of the "Decisive Decade," 1954–1964.* New York: Herder & Herder, Inc., 1965. 282 pp.

Contains six bibliographic essays by prominent Catholic scholars on theological trends, Old Testament and New Testament studies, patristic studies, liturgical studies, and theology in transition during a decade of rapid change. Each essay also has appended a classified bibliography of works published during the same period. Subject index and name index included.

CURRENT BIBLIOGRAPHY

While retrospective bibliographies are completed when published (although new editions may be issued from time to time), current bibliographies are ongoing and continuous and usually take the form of indexing and abstracting journals. Such "serialized bibliographies" are issued at regular intervals, some annually, others several times a year. Of course, the shorter the time lag between the publication of the current issue of the bibliography and the date of publication of the material being indexed, the better the tool.

Some current bibliographies index only periodicals, while others include books also. Some also have book review sections. Some may provide abstracts or résumés of the materials treated, while others simply cite the work itself and let the title or subject heading give the clue as to whether or not it supplies the informational needs of the researcher. Some such tools, often European in origin, are arranged in classified order, while others, usually American, are arranged in alphabetical, or dictionary, order. The tools listed here cover the whole spectrum of theological inquiry. Those specifically designed for such areas as Biblical studies, history, or missions will be cited with other works under these chapter headings. The student whose language mastery is limited to English should not neglect using indexing tools that have German, French, or Latin titles, as these invariably list many English language works also. A more complete listing of foreign-language indexing services will be found in Schwinge (no. 19), pp. 63–64.

Theological Indexes and Abstracts

42. "Elenchus Bibliographicus" in *Ephemerides Theologicae Lovanienses.* University of Louvain. Gembloux: Duculot, 1924 to date. Quarterly.

The most complete serialized bibliography in the field of theology. "Elenchus bibliographicus" (Bibliographical record) is a section of the journal *Ephemerides Theologicae Lovanienses* (Louvain Theological Review). This ecumenically oriented Belgian Catholic work lists scholarly books, book reviews, articles, and pamphlets annually in classified order under the headings: generalia, historia religionum, scriptura sacra Veteris Testamenti, scriptura sacra Novi Testamenti, theologia fundamentalis, theologia dogmatica specialis, theologia sacramentorum, theologia ascetico-mystica, theologia moralis, jus canonicum. Author index only. Includes many titles in English. Latin subject headings for classification system are not difficult for English-speaking students to understand.

43. American Theological Library Association. *Index to Religious Periodical Literature;* an author and subject index to periodical literature, including an author index to book reviews. 1949/1952 to date. Chicago: American Theological Library Association, 1953 to date. Semiannual with cumulation every two years.

This tool is the first place to start when looking for English-language periodical literature in theology and related disciplines. It indexes some 200 theological journals from many countries, mostly in English and generally Protestant, although some Catholic and Jewish periodicals are included. It is now beginning to provide abstracts for some of the articles indexed. Since 1975 each issue has been divided into three sections: subject index, author index with abstracts, and book review index. Previously there was a combined subject-author index and a book review index. Since this publication now appears in a computer-compiled format, entries for the Bible appear in alphabetical order rather than canonical order under the heading "Bible." Thus, the subject heading "Bible (NT)" is listed before "Bible (OT)." With the July-Dec. 1977 semiannual issue the name *IRPL* was changed to *Religious Index One: Periodicals.* In 1978, *Religious Index Two: Multi-Author Works* began indexing Festschriften, collections of essays, and other scholarly, multiauthor studies in theology and related fields with 1976 imprints in English and Western European languages.

44. *Religious and Theological Abstracts.* March 1958 to date. Myerstown, Pa.: Religious and Theological Abstracts, 1958 to date. Quarterly.

Each issue has abstracts of selected articles from over 150 primarily Protestant English-language journals, arranged in classified order under the headings: Biblical, theological, historical, practical, sociological. No cumulations, but annual cumulated subject, author, and Scripture indexes are provided.

45. *Scripta Recenter Edita; International Current Bibliography of Books Published in the Fields of Philosophical and Theological Sciences.* Nijmegen: World Library Service, 1959 to date. Quarterly.

Each issue is arranged in classified order. Has annual cumulated index of authors and anonymous works. Over 7,000 titles are listed annually in several languages. Published by Dutch and Belgian Catholic librarians.

46. *Christian Periodical Index* (a selected list); an index to subjects, authors, and book reviews. 1956/1960 to date. Buffalo: Christian Librarians' Fellowship, 1961 to date. Quarterly with annual and five-year cumulations.

Indexes over 40 scholarly and popular journals, primarily American and evangelical.

47. Richardson, Ernest Cushing. *An Alphabetical Subject Index and Index Encyclopaedia to Periodical Articles on Religion, 1890–1899.* New York: Charles Scribner's Sons, 1907–1911. 2 vols.

Indexes 58,000 articles by 21,000 writers in more than 600 periodicals in English and other Western European languages. The subject volume includes definitions of the subject headings used and identification of persons with references to encyclopedia articles. The author volume indexes the same works as the subject volume.

48. Regazzi, John J., and Hines, Theodore C. *A Guide to Indexed Periodicals in Religion.* Metuchen, N.J.: Scarecrow Press, Inc., 1975. 314 pp.

A computer-produced work indicating where some 2,700 periodicals in religion are indexed in seventeen abstracting and indexing services.

OTHER INDEXES AND ABSTRACTS

In addition to the theological periodical indexes, the theological student should also be familiar with the other related periodical indexes listed below. These are invaluable tools without which the literature appearing in periodicals would be buried, lost, and largely forgotten. Libraries do not normally catalog separately articles appearing in periodicals. Often periodicals will provide their own indexes, cumulated on an annual, five-year, or ten-year basis. However, finding periodical articles through such means requires the tedium of going through many, many indexes. The indexes listed in this section index scores or even hundreds of journals in a single alphabetical sequence, usually including both authors and subjects. The trend today, especially for the more scholarly subject-indexing services, is to provide also abstracts or résumés of the articles indexed.

49. *Readers' Guide to Periodical Literature.* 1900 to date. New York: The H. W. Wilson Company, 1905 to date.

Indexes by subject, author, and—when necessary—title, articles in U.S. popular, nontechnical, news, and opinion journals. Issued semimonthly with annual and longer cumulations. Useful for indexing to *The Christian Century,* which does not appear in *Index to Religious Periodical Literature* (no. 43) until 1971. For indexing of nineteenth-century periodical literature it is necessary to use the following:

50. *Poole's Index to Periodical Literature,* 1802–1881. Rev. ed., Boston: Houghton, 1891. 2 vols. (Reprint: New York: Peter Smith, 1938; Gloucester, Mass.: Peter Smith, 1963).

————. Supplements, Jan. 1882–Jan. 1, 1907. Boston: Houghton, 1887–1908. 5 vols.

Subject index only. Author access to *Poole's* is now provided by:

51. Wall, C. Edward. *Cumulative Author Index for Poole's Index to Periodical Literature, 1802–1906.* Ann Arbor: Pierian Press, 1971. 488 pp.

52. *Nineteenth Century Readers' Guide to Periodical Literature, 1890–1899,* with supplementary indexing, 1900–1922. The H. W. Wilson Company, 1944. 2 vols.

Indexes mainly literary and general periodicals. The two volumes were the beginning of a project, never completed, to index nineteenth-century periodical literature by modern indexing standards.

53. *Humanities Index.* June 1974 to date. The H. W. Wilson Company, 1974 to date. Quarterly with annual cumulations.

An author-subject index of 260 scholarly journals, U.S. and foreign. "Subject fields indexed include archaeology and classical studies, area studies, folklore, history, language and literature, literary and political criticism, performing arts, philosophy, religion and theology, and related subjects" (Prefatory Note, Vol. 1). Previously part of *Social Sciences and Humanities Index,* which was earlier entitled *International Index to Periodicals* (1907/1915–1974).

54. *Social Sciences Index.* June 1974 to date. New York: The H. W. Wilson Company, 1974 to date. Quarterly with annual cumulations.

An author-subject index of 263 scholarly journals in the fields of "anthropology, area studies, economics, environmental science, geography, law and criminology, medical sciences, political science, psychology, public administration, sociology and related subjects" (Prefatory Note, Vol. 2). Previously part of *Social Sciences and Humanities Index,* which was earlier entitled *International Index to Periodicals* (1907/1915–1974).

55. *British Humanities Index.* 1962 to date. London: The Library Association, 1963 to date. Quarterly, with annual cumulations.

Attempts to cover "all material relating to the arts and politics." Indexes 380 British periodicals.

56. *The Philosopher's Index;* an international index to philosophical periodicals. Spring 1967 to date. Bowling Green, Ohio: Bowling Green University, 1967 to date. Quarterly, with annual cumulations.

Covers "all major American and British philosophical periodicals, selected journals in other languages, and related interdisciplinary publications." Since 1969 has included abstracts of many articles indexed.

57. *Psychological Abstracts.* 1927 to date. Lancaster, Pa.: American Psychological Association, 1927 to date. Monthly.

Indexes and abstracts new books and journal articles by subject. Monthly issues contain author index; annual cumulation has complete author and subject indexes.

58. *Sociological Abstracts.* Nov. 1952 to date. New York: Sociological Abstracts, 1952 to date.

Frequency varies; now published six times a year. Provides

abstracts from both U.S. and foreign periodicals; arranged in classified order.

59. *Education Index,* a cumulative subject index to a selected list of educational periodicals, proceedings, and yearbooks. Jan. 1929 to date. The H. W. Wilson Company, 1932 to date. Monthly (except July and Aug.), cumulating throughout the year, with annual bound cumulation.

Indexes about 240 periodicals, proceedings, yearbooks, etc. Since 1961 indexed by subject only; previously by subject and author.

60. Public Affairs Information Service. *Bulletin of the Public Affairs Information Service.* Annual cumulations. New York, 1915 to date.

Often cited as *PAIS.* Selectively indexes over 1,000 journals in English, plus government documents, books, pamphlets, and reports in the fields of political science, legislation, sociology, and economics.

Among the few indexes for newspapers are:

61. *The New York Times Index.* 1913 to date. New York, 1913 to date. Semimonthly, with annual cumulation.

A subject index giving date, page, and column references. Indexes the Late City edition, which is available on microfilm in many libraries. A most useful tool for locating information on specific events, speeches, documents, or persons.

62. Christian Science Monitor. *Index to the Christian Science Monitor.* Jan. 1960 to date. Boston, 1960 to date. Monthly, with semiannual and annual cumulations.

SERIAL AND PERIODICAL DIRECTORIES

The *Anglo-American Cataloging Rules* (Chicago: American Library Association, 1967, p. 346) defines "serial" as: "A publication issued in successive parts bearing numerical or chronological designations and intended to be continued indefinitely. Serials include periodicals, newspapers, annuals (reports, yearbooks, etc.), the journals, memoirs, proceedings, transactions, etc., of societies, and numbered monographic series." The same work (p. 345) defines "periodical" as: "A serial appearing or intended to appear indefinitely at regular or stated intervals, generally more frequently than annually, each issue of which normally contains separate articles, stories, or other writings. Newspapers disseminating general news, and the proceedings, papers, or other publications of corporate bodies primarily related to their meetings are not included in this term."

From this it is apparent that the term "serial" is more inclusive than "periodical." Listed below are directories of currently published irregular serials and annuals, of periodicals (which are serials published more than once a year), and of newspapers. Such directories provide the following types of information: exact title, publisher's name and address, circulation, subscription cost, where indexed, etc.

63. *Irregular Serials and Annuals; An International Directory.* A classified guide to current foreign and domestic serials, excepting periodicals issued more frequently than once a year. New York: R. R. Bowker Company, 1967 to date. Biennial (beginning 1972).

The place to look for bibliographic information on such works as publications of societies, e.g., bulletins, proceedings, transactions, newsletters, yearbooks, directories, and annuals, as well as monographic series. Contains title-subject index and cross-index to subjects. This work is a companion volume to Ulrich's (no. 64).

64. *Ulrich's International Periodicals Directory;* a classified guide to periodicals, foreign and domestic. New York: R. R. Bowker Company, 1932 to date. Biennial.

The 17th ed., published 1977, contains bibliographic information on over 60,000 current periodical titles from throughout the world. Has separate list for ceased publications for the previous two-year period. Contains title index and cross-index to subjects.

65. *The Standard Periodical Directory.* 1964/65 to date. New York: Oxbridge Publishing Co., Inc., 1964. Irregular.

Lists over 62,000 U.S. and Canadian periodicals. Arranged alphabetically within subjects. Contains title index. Along with usual bibliographic information, it also gives editorial content and scope, year founded, frequency, advertising rate, etc.

66. *Ayer Directory of Publications.* Philadelphia: Ayer Press, 1880 to date. Maps. Annual.

Strives to publish "the most current, accurate, and useful information relating to newspapers, magazines, trade and professional publications" that appear at least four times a year. Arranged geographically by states, alphabetically by cities within states. Lists advertising rates and circulation statistics, as well as general gazetteer information about each state, province, city, and town listed; 19 classified lists and 68 specially made maps.

Union Lists of Serials

A union list of serials attempts to list both currently published as well as ceased serials, and also indicates various libraries where each serial may be found. While libraries usually will not lend serials through Interlibrary Loan, they will make photocopies of particular articles for a reasonable charge.

67. *Union List of Serials in Libraries in the United States and Canada.* 3d ed. Edited by Edna Brown Titus. New York: The H. W. Wilson Company, 1965. 5 vols. (4,649 pp.)

1st ed., 1927.

Lists over 156,000 serials published before 1950 and held by 956 cooperating libraries. Gives the exact holdings information of each library having a particular serial. Does not include newspapers after 1820. The first place to go to locate an issue of a particular journal, domestic or foreign, except journals in Far Eastern languages.

68. *New Serial Titles;* a union list of serials commencing publication after Dec. 31, 1949. Washington: Library of Congress, Jan. 1953 to date. Monthly with annual cumulations.

———. 1950–1970 cumulation. Washington: Library of Congress; New York: R. R. Bowker Company, 1973. 4 vols.

Continues *Union List of Serials* (no. 67) in monthly issues; cumulated annually and every five, ten, and twenty years.

69. Center for Research Libraries, Chicago. *The Center for Research Libraries Catalogue: Serials.* Chicago: The Center, 1972. 2 vols.

The Center for Research Libraries—whose membership comprises over 100 major research libraries—acquires, stores, and makes available infrequently used, though important, research materials. Materials are available only through member libraries. Serials, including newspapers, cataloged through April 1971 are contained in the catalog.

70. Brigham, Clarence S. *History and Bibliography of American Newspapers, 1690–1820.* Worcester, Mass.: American Antiquarian Society, 1947. 2 vols. (Reprint: Hamden, Conn.: Archon Books, 1962. 2 vols. including Additions and Corrections.)

Lists 2,120 newspapers by state and alphabetically by locality within each state. Indicates detailed bibliographic history of each paper and location in libraries throughout the United States. A most important work for historical research; required fifteen years to complete.

71. *International Congresses and Conferences, 1840–1937;* a union list of the publications available in libraries of the United States and Canada, ed. by Winifred Gregory under the auspices of the Bibliographical Society of America . . . New York: The H. W. Wilson Company, 1938. 229 pp.

In addition to general union lists of serials, there are also regional union lists of serials for theological libraries, such as the following:

72. Chicago Area Theological Library Association. *Union List of Serials.* 1st ed. Chicago, 1974. 673 pp.

Serial titles, excluding annuals and monographic series, are listed alphabetically by title with indication of holdings from twenty-two (17 Protestant, 5 Catholic) seminaries in the Chicago area. Includes many titles not found in the *Union List of Serials in Libraries in the United States and Canada* (no. 67).

73. Boston Theological Institute. *Union List of Periodicals;* preliminary checking ed. Boston, 1974. 409 pp.

Reports holdings of eight theological schools in the Boston area.

For the *Union List of United Methodist Serials,* see no. 437.

NATIONAL AND TRADE BIBLIOGRAPHIES

Listed here are a few of the reference tools for finding currently published books in the United States, Great Britain,

France, and Germany. In addition to these works, the massive library catalogs of the Library of Congress, the British Museum, and the Bibliothèque Nationale (nos. 30–35), and especially their more recent supplements, should be consulted.

74. *Publishers' Trade List Annual.* 1873 to date. New York: R. R. Bowker Company, 1873 to date. Annual.

Often cited as *PTLA,* this multivolume work is simply a compilation of American publishers' catalogs in alphabetical order by the publishers' names. The amount of bibliographic detail varies depending on the particular publisher's catalog. A list of publishers appears in the first volume. Contains only in-print books.

75. *Books in Print.* 1948 to date. New York: R. R. Bowker Company, 1948 to date. Annual.

This work was formerly subtitled "An author-title-series index to the Publishers' Trade List Annual" (see no. 74). Coverage has now been expanded "to include information from additional publishers whose titles were not included in *PTLA.*" Appears in four volumes: two listing works by authors in alphabetical order and two listing works by titles in alphabetical order. Publishers and prices given. Useful for finding bibliographic information if only an author or only the title of a book is known. Usually available for use in bookstores as well as libraries.

76. *Subject Guide to Books in Print.* 1957 to date. New York: R. R. Bowker Company, 1957 to date. Annual.

Arranges titles listed in *Books in Print* (no. 75) by subject, using the subject headings and cross-references of the Library of Congress system. Works for which the Library of Congress does not assign subject headings, such as Bibles, fiction, poetry, and drama, are not listed. See no. 33 for a thesaurus of the Library of Congress subject headings.

77. *Cumulative Book Index; A World List of Books in the English Language.* 1928/32 to date. New York: The H. W. Wilson Company, 1933 to date.

Often cited as *CBI,* now published monthly with various cumulations: biennial beginning in 1957, annual since 1969. A "dictionary listing" by author, title, and subject of books in English printed in the United States and Canada as well as selected titles from other parts of the English-speaking world, such as

Australia, Great Britain, New Zealand, South Africa, etc.

78. *British Books in Print; The Reference Catalogue of Current Literature* . ... 1965 to date. London: J. Whitaker & Sons, Ltd., 1965 to date.

Vol. 1, authors; Vol. 2, titles.

79. *British National Bibliography.* 1950 to date. London: Council of the British National Bibliography, British Museum, 1950 to date.

Published weekly with four cumulations a year as well as an annual and a five-year cumulation. Attempts to list most works published in Great Britain. Arranged by subject according to the Dewey Decimal Classification. Includes author-title index, subject index, and list of British publishers. Used with *Subject Guide to Books in Print* (no. 76) and *Cumulative Book Index* (no. 77), it provides thorough coverage of current books in English in any field of interest.

80. *Verzeichnis lieferbarer Bücher.* 1970 to date. Frankfurt am Main: Verlag der Buchhändler-Vereinigung GmbH, 1970 to date.

The German "Books in Print." An annual listing of books currently available from German, Austrian, and Swiss publishers. Authors, titles, series, and key words arranged alphabetically in one sequence.

81. *Les Livres de l'Année—Biblio.* 1971 to date. Paris, Cercle de la Librairie, 1972 to date. Annual. Continues *Biblio,* 1934–1970.

Includes books published in France as well as those in French published in Switzerland, Belgium, Canada, etc. Author-title-subject dictionary arrangement.

REPRINT AND MICROFORM CATALOGS

While many older works are usually out of print, they can often be found in reprinted editions, either in hard copy or in microfilm (roll form) or microfiche (card form). Listed below are catalogs of such reprinted works.

82. *Guide to Reprints.* 1967 to date. Englewood, Colo.: Information Handling Services, Library and Education Division, 1967 to date. Annual.

"An annual cumulative guide, in alphabetic order, to books, journals, and other materials, which are available in reprint form" (Preface). Includes works of over 300 publishers.

83. *Guide to Microforms in Print.* 1961 to date. Englewood, Colo.: Information Handling Services, Library and Education Division, 1961 to date. Annual.

"An annual, cumulative guide, in alphabetic order, to books, journals, and other materials which are available on microfilm or other microforms from United States publishers" (Preface). Lists works of over 100 publishers, including the American Theological Library Association's Board of Microtext since 1976, the Presbyterian Historical Society, and the American Jewish Periodical Center.

84. *National Register of Microform Masters.* Comp. by the Library of Congress with the cooperation of the American Library Association and the Association of Research Libraries. Washington: Library of Congress, Sept. 1965 to date. Irregular, then annual.

Lists master microform copies owned and preserved by non-profit institutions. If copyright permits, positive copies for readers' use are usually available. "The *Register* reports master microforms of foreign and domestic books, pamphlets, serials, and foreign and domestic archival manuscript collections, U.S. doctoral dissertations, and masters' theses. . . . Each (annual) edition presents new reports and does not supersede any previous issues" (Foreword).

TRANSLATIONS

In a large theological research library, the reader may be surprised to discover that 40 percent or more of the books and journals currently acquired are in German. Consequently, the following bibliographies may be of special interest to theological. students and teachers.

85. *Bibliographie der Übersetzungen deutschsprachiger Werke.* Verzeichnis der in der Deutschen Bücherei eingegangenen Schriften, bearb. und hrsg. von der Deutschen Bücherei. Leipzig: Verlag für Buch- und Bibliothekswesen, 1954 to date. Quarterly.

48   *The Literature of Theology*

A bibliography of German works translated into other languages. Arranged by language and then in classified order under each language. Includes indexes by subject, author, and publisher. The translated title is followed by the German title in parentheses.

86. *Index Translationum. Répertoire International des Traductions. International Bibliography of Translations.* Paris: International Institute of Intellectual Cooperation, 1932–1940, Nos. 1–31. New series, 1948 to date. Paris: UNESCO, 1949 to date. Annual.

Includes works from over 75 countries. Arranged by country and by subject within country. Provides indexes of authors, publishers, and translators.

FESTSCHRIFTEN

"Festschrift" is the German word for a memorial or homage work honoring a scholar, an institution, or a special event. Such a work, published either separately or as part of a journal, consists of a collection of scholarly articles. Unfortunately, many such articles in theological Festschriften remain buried for want of adequate indexes. In 1978 *Religious Index Two: Multi-Author Works* began publishing an annual index for Festschriften, collections of essays, and other scholarly, multiauthor studies in theology and related fields for 1976 and later imprints in English and Western European languages (see no. 43). Listed below are some other recent efforts to provide retrospective indexing for theological Festschriften.

87. O'Brien, Betty Alice, and O'Brien, Elmer John. *A Bibliography of Festschriften in Religion Published Since 1960;* a preliminary checklist. Dayton, Ohio, 1975. No paging.

Lists in chronological order by year and alphabetical order by person, institution, or event honored approximately 1,500 Festschriften published from 1960 to 1974. Does not provide an index by author or subject to articles contained in these Festschriften.

88. Sayre, John L., and Hamburger, Roberta. *An Index of Festschriften in Religion in the Graduate Seminary Library of Phillips University.* Enid, Okla.: Haymaker, 1970. 121 pp.

Indexes by author and subject 84 volumes of Festschriften.

89. ———, ———. *An Index of Festschriften in Religion: New Titles, 1971–1973, in the Graduate Seminary Library of Phillips University.* Enid, Okla.: Seminary Press, 1973. 136 pp.

Indexes an additional 71 volumes of Festschriften in this particular library.

See also nos. 249, 453.

DISSERTATIONS AND THESES

The term "dissertation" is now used to refer to the research paper done as part of the doctoral degree work, while "thesis" applies to the written project for the master's degree.

90. *Dissertation Abstracts International.* Ann Arbor, Mich.: University Microfilms, 1938 to date. Monthly with annual cumulated author and subject index.

Consists of abstracts of doctoral dissertations submitted by over 240 U.S. and Canadian universities; classified arrangement with key-word title index and author index. Part IV of the A Section (Humanities) is Philosophy, Religion, and Theology. A hard copy or microfilm copy of any dissertation listed may be ordered from University Microfilms at a moderate cost.

91. *Comprehensive Dissertation Index: 1861–1972.* Ann Arbor, Mich.: Xerox University Microfilms, 1973. 37 vols.

Has separate volumes for the various subjects, e.g., Vol. 32, Philosophy and Religion. Vols. 33–37 contain an author index for the whole work. Within volumes, entries are arranged alphabetically by key words in the dissertation titles. Bibliographic information and reference to *Dissertation Abstracts International* or other lists are cited.

92. Council on Graduate Studies in Religion. *Doctoral Dissertations in the Field of Religion, 1940–1952.* Includes title, location, field, and a short précis of contents. New York: Columbia University Press, 1954. 194 pp.

Arranged alphabetically by author. Supplement to *Review of Religion,* Vol. 18. Includes 425 dissertations and provides a brief abstract for each.

———. ———. Supplement. 1952 to date. Annual. Title

varies, but from 1964 onward called *Dissertation Title Index.* Arranged alphabetically by author and usually lists works in progress.

For dissertations in religious education, see no. 472.

MANUSCRIPTS

93. *National Union Catalog of Manuscript Collections.* 1959/61 to date. Hamden, Conn.: Shoe String Press, 1962 to date. Annual.

The basic locating guide for historical manuscripts in U.S. repositories. "Since its beginning this catalog has published descriptions of approximately 35,500 collections located in 950 different repositories and has indexed them by approximately 350,280 references to topical subjects and personal, family, corporate and geographical names" (Preface). Index is published annually and cumulated each year through a five-year period.

GOVERNMENT PUBLICATIONS

The United States Government is the largest publisher in the world, and yet "Government documents," as they are sometimes called, are not fully utilized because they are controlled by a completely different bibliographic system than the familiar cataloging treatment used for books in academic or public libraries. However, clergy or lay persons involved in social concerns ought to be aware of the vast resources of information and documentation in Government publications, especially in such areas as housing, welfare, economics, labor, industry, ecology, statistics, education, international affairs, history, and any other area touched by governmental concern.

Physical access to Government publications is available to any citizen through an official Government depository, at least one of which is located in each Congressional district. Often such depositories are housed in college or university libraries.

Listed below are both a general guide to the whole field of Government documents and the basic bibliographic tool for providing access to this ever-increasing flow of publications.

94. Schmeckebier, Laurence Frederick, and Eastin, Roy B.

Government Publications and Their Use. 2d rev. ed. Washington: The Brookings Institution, 1969. 502 pp.

A useful, detailed guide.

95. U.S. Superintendent of Documents. *Monthly Catalog of United States Government Publications.* 1895 to date. Washington: Government Printing Office, 1898 to date. Monthly.

A current bibliography of publications by all branches of government, with monthly and annual indexes. Each document is identified with a unique number that serves as the classification number for storage and retrieval in all Government documents depositories as well as the order number to be used when purchasing a copy.

CHAPTER II

Encyclopedias and Dictionaries

Encyclopedias, both general and specialized, are the basic reference tools in either a personal or institutional library. A good encyclopedia should be used to find three different types of material: (1) factual information; (2) comprehensive, summary discussions of specific subjects including current views and often historical development; (3) bibliography for more in-depth topical study.

Sometimes the reader needs only simple factual information, such as the biographical details of Jonathan Edwards, a résumé of his major works, and a discussion of the place he occupies in American intellectual and ecclesiastical history. Or the reader may need a bibliography of selected, authoritative works on Edwards to pursue a more in-depth study. A good encyclopedia should be able to fulfill these three needs: the factual, the educational, and the bibliographic. While readers often turn to an encyclopedia for the first two, many are unaware of its value for the third, the bibliographic.

However, some readers have developed a definite bias against using an encyclopedia at all. This near-phobia may stem from an early elementary or secondary school experience where the teacher warned against using an encyclopedia in a writing assignment lest the text be copied verbatim and at length. Or it may result from the mistaken notion that an encyclopedia article can, of necessity, provide only superficial treatment of any subject because its articles are shorter than monographs on the same subject. But encyclopedias that are well written by recognized subject specialists and carefully edited provide compendiums of fact, thought, and bibliography on the whole universe of knowledge. And special subject encyclopedias on theology and the other disciplines, such as those listed below, are works that neither student nor scholar will ever outgrow.

For a more detailed discussion of encyclopedias and standards for evaluating and purchasing them, see Sheehy (no. 1), pp. 97–99, or Robert Collison, *Encyclopaedias: Their History Throughout the Ages* (New York and London: Hafner Publishing Company, Inc., 1964).

Often the terms "encyclopedia" and "dictionary" are used interchangeably, but generally "encyclopedia" refers to a work with longer, in-depth articles whereas "dictionary" refers to a work with shorter, more concise, definition-style articles.

THEOLOGICAL ENCYCLOPEDIAS AND DICTIONARIES

Included here are both multivolume encyclopedias and single-volume dictionaries that cover theology, church history, Bible, biography, and, to varying extents, non-Christian religions. Encyclopedias or dictionaries dealing primarily with the Bible or with a particular denomination or confession, or primarily with theology proper, will be found listed with the other works covering these same subjects.

96. *Encyclopaedia of Religion and Ethics;* ed. by James Hastings, with the assistance of John A. Selbie and Louis H. Gray. Edinburgh: T. & T. Clark; New York: Charles Scribner's Sons, 1908–1927. 12 vols. and index. (Reprint: Charles Scribner's Sons, 1959.)

Old, but still not superseded. Contains long, signed articles with bibliography, covering Christian and all other religions, as well as related subjects in mythology, folklore, anthropology, psychology, and sociology. Includes names of persons and places.

97. *Schaff-Herzog Encyclopedia. The New Schaff-Herzog Encyclopedia of Religious Knowledge.* S. M. Jackson, ed. in chief. New York: Funk & Wagnalls, 1908–1912. 12 vols. and index. (Reprint: Grand Rapids, Mich.: Baker Book House, 1949–1950. 13 vols.)

One of the most important and comprehensive Protestant-oriented theological encyclopedias in English. Covers theology, church history, Bible, denominations and sects, missions. Contains bibliographic survey in the preface (Vol. 1, pp. xii– xiv), a bibliographic appendix at the beginning of each volume, and bibliographies appended to each article. Based on 3d ed. of the Herzog-Hauck *Realencyklopädie,* although not a translation of that work, but a condensation and updating of it for the American reader. More recently brought up to date by the following:

98. *Twentieth Century Encyclopedia of Religious Knowledge:* an extension of The New Schaff-Herzog Encyclopedia of Religious Knowledge. Lefferts A. Loetscher, ed. in chief. Grand Rapids, Mich.: Baker Book House, 1955. 2 vols. 1,205 pp.

Signed articles, with bibliographies, covering newer subjects and persons, both living and dead at the time of publication.

99. *The Oxford Dictionary of the Christian Church.* 2d ed., ed. by F. L. Cross and E. A. Livingstone. London: Oxford University Press, 1974. 1,518 pp.

1st ed., 1957.

An outstanding one-volume work with up-to-date articles on people, movements, churches, societies, and doctrines, with bibliographies attached to most articles. Anglican in orientation. A reference tool of immeasurable value to student, pastor, teacher, and librarian.

100. *Corpus Dictionary of Western Churches.* T. C. O'Brien, ed. Washington and Cleveland: Corpus Publications, 1970. 820 pp.

"Is a reference volume on the churches that have developed throughout the history of Western Christianity. Special attention is given to North American Churches in the Western tradition that are of either historical or contemporary significance, particularly those reported in the National Council of Churches' *Yearbook of American Churches* (1969)" (Preface). Stronger on history of the churches than on doctrinal issues. The editor is Catholic, although most of the contributors are members of the churches about which they write. Includes biographical sketches and bibliography with the more important articles. A useful supplement to *The Oxford Dictionary of the Christian Church* (no. 99).

101. Douglas, J.D., ed. *The New International Dictionary of*

the Christian Church. Zondervan Publishing House, 1974. 1,074 pp.

A comprehensive work, strong in church history and biography. Signed articles with bibliographies appended. Represents British and American conservative Protestant perspective.

GENERAL ENCYCLOPEDIAS

102. *Encyclopedia Americana.* New York and Chicago: Encyclopedia Americana. 30 vols.

Like many other contemporary encyclopedias, the *Americana* is continuously revised so that each new printing contains some new or revised articles. Thus, there are no longer whole new editions as such when this policy prevails. The *Americana* is a comprehensive, reliable work with signed articles. Bibliographies are not always up-to-date. As in most encyclopedias, use of the index, in this case, Vol. 30, is the easiest, quickest, and surest way to find all the information desired.

103. *Encyclopaedia Britannica.* 15th ed. Chicago: Encyclopaedia Britannica, 1974. 30 vols.

Contents: Propaedia, outline of knowledge and guide to the *Britannica,* 1 vol.; Micropaedia, 10 vols.; Macropaedia, 19 vols.

Now published in the United States, this most famous of English-language encyclopedias began in Great Britain in 1768. In its early editions it was essentially a collection of long, scholarly monographs. The 9th ed. (1875–1889) represents the height of this scholarly tradition. Later editions provide shorter articles under more numerous subject headings. The policy of "continuous revision" since the 14th ed., 1929, was abandoned and an entirely new edition, based on a new plan, was brought out with the 15th ed. in 1974. The informational and quick-reference function is provided by shorter articles in the ten volumes of the "Micropaedia." The educational function is provided by the more in-depth articles in the "Macropaedia" as well as by the outlines and discussions of the whole universe of knowledge, arranged in classified order, in the "Propaedia." The "Micropaedia" also serves as an index to the longer articles in the "Macropaedia."

104. *The New Columbia Encyclopedia.* 4th ed. New York:

Columbia University Press, 1975. 3,052 pp.

1st ed., 1935.

A concise, well-written one-volume work that is especially useful when exhaustive articles are not needed. Provides brief, up-to-date bibliographies.

SUBJECT ENCYCLOPEDIAS

Some of the standard subject encyclopedias that may often be of special interest to the student of theology are:

105. *Dictionary of the History of Ideas;* studies of selected pivotal ideas. Philip P. Wiener, ed. in chief. New York: Charles Scribner's Sons, 1973–1974. 4 vols. and index.

Contains longer, signed articles by specialists who attempt to show the historical interrelationships of ideas, "to help establish some sense of the unity of human thought and its cultural manifestations in a world of ever-increasing specialization and alienation" (Preface). Arranged in alphabetical order by subjects. Bibliographies appended to each article. Vol. 5 consists of a topical index, which is essential for using this work as the same subject is often discussed in a variety of ways in many different articles.

106. *Encyclopedia of Philosophy.* Paul Edwards, ed. in chief. New York: The Macmillan Company, 1967. 8 vols.

Signed articles often of considerable length, including bibliographies, arranged in alphabetical order by subject. Aims "to cover the whole of philosophy and other disciplines. The *Encyclopedia* treats Eastern and Western philosophy; it deals with ancient, medieval and modern philosophy; and it discusses the theories of mathematicians, physicists, biologists, sociologists, psychologists, moral reformers, and religious thinkers where these have had an impact on philosophy" (Introduction). Useful for both the specialist and the nonspecialist. Vol. 8 is the index.

107. *Encyclopaedia of the Social Sciences.* E. R. A. Seligman, ed. in chief; Alvin Johnson, assoc. ed. New York: The Macmillan Company, 1930–1935. 15 vols.

A comprehensive, older work that is still useful. Descriptive and historical in approach. About half of its articles are biographical.

108. *International Encyclopedia of the Social Sciences.* David L. Sills, ed. New York: The Macmillan Company and The Free Press, 1968. 17 vols.

Not a revision of the earlier work (no. 107), but entirely new. "Designed to complement, not to supplant, its predecessor" (Introduction). The topical articles cover anthropology, economics, geography, history, law, political science, psychiatry, psychology, sociology, and statistics. Main emphasis is on the analytical and comparative rather than on the historical and descriptive. Contains biographies of six hundred persons rather than four thousand as in the earlier work. Bibliographies appended to each article. Use of the index is essential.

109. *Encyclopedia of Social Work.* 17th issue. John B. Turner, ed. in chief. New York: National Association of Social Workers, 1977. 2 vols.

Successor to the *Social Work Year Book,* 1929–1960. Current edition contains some 200 articles and 100 biographies; arranged in alphabetical order. Bibliographies and cross-references with many articles. Index included.

110. *Encyclopedia of Psychology.* H. J. Eysenck, W. Arnold, and R. Meili, eds. London: Search Press; New York: Herder & Herder, Inc., 1972. 3 vols.

An international work published in English, German, French, Spanish, Portuguese, and Italian, although it "presents psychology as increasingly understood and accepted in the English-speaking world" (Prefatory Note). Contains both shorter definitions as well as longer, signed articles ranging up to 4,000 words. Many articles contain selective bibliographies. No index. Useful for both specialist and layperson.

111. *Encyclopedia of Mental Health.* Albert Deutsch, ed. New York: Franklin Watts, Inc., 1963. 6 vols.

Consists of 170 articles in question-and-answer form, arranged alphabetically by topic. Written by specialists for the layperson. Vol. 6 includes bibliography, index, glossary, and list of agencies.

112. *Encyclopedia of Education.* Lee C. Deighton, ed. in chief. New York: The Macmillan Company and The Free Press, 1971. 10 vols.

Treats education in the widest sense. Contains longer articles, most of which have bibliographies appended. Arranged alphabetically. An enlarged "Guide to Articles" appears in Vol. 9. The index, Vol. 10, is absolutely essential as it "contains not only the usual topical references but groupings of articles under conceptual headings" (Preface).

113. *Encyclopedia of World Art.* New York: McGraw-Hill Book Co., Inc., 1959–1964. 15 vols.

Published simultaneously in Italian and English. A massive work consisting of "an articulated collection of organic monographic studies of limited number and sufficient length to develop their content with the desired completeness" (Preface). Arranged alphabetically with the final volume an "analytic dictionary index." Profusely illustrated with both colored and black-and-white plates. Treats art in the broadest sense, including architecture, sculpture, and painting of all countries and all periods. Bibliographies in the English edition have been amplified for the English-speaking reader.

114. Grove, (Sir) George. *Dictionary of Music and Musicians.* 5th ed. Eric Blom, ed. New York: St. Martin's Press, 1955. 9 vols.

The standard work on music for the period from 1450 onward. Strong British emphasis. Bibliographies include periodical articles.

―――. ―――. Supplementary volume. St. Martin's Press, 1961. 492 pp.

115. *Van Nostrand's Scientific Encyclopedia.* 5th ed. New York: Van Nostrand Reinhold, 1976. 2,370 pp.

Short articles without bibliography. Useful to the layperson as well as the specialist. The layperson can also profitably use one of the good juvenile encyclopedias for scientific articles. See Sheehy (no. 1), pp. 101–102.

ENGLISH-LANGUAGE DICTIONARIES

Among the outstanding American and British dictionaries are:

116. *Webster's New International Dictionary of the English Language.* 2d ed., unabridged. Springfield, Mass.: G. & C. Merriam Company, 1961. 3,194 pp.

This edition, first published in 1934 and slightly revised in later printings, serves as the American authority for the English language, even though it is now out of print.

117. *Webster's Third New International Dictionary of the English Language, Unabridged.* Springfield, Mass.: G. & C. Merriam Company, 1961. 2,662 pp.

An extremely controversial work when first published because it did not claim authority for correctness, but instead tried to reflect current usage. Consequently, much that would be considered as colloquial, slang, or even vulgar was included. Total entries were reduced from 600,000 in the 2d ed. to 450,000 in the 3d ed., although 100,000 new entries appear in the latter work.

118. Murray, (Sir) James Augustus Henry. *Oxford English Dictionary,* being a corrected reissue, with an introduction, supplement and bibliography, of A New English Dictionary on Historical Principles; founded mainly on the materials collected by the Philological Society and ed. by James A. H. Murray, Henry Bradley, W. A. Craigie, C. T. Onions. Oxford: Clarendon Press, 1933. 12 vols. and supplement.

A reprint of the *New English Dictionary,* 1888–1933. Often cited as the O.E.D. A 2-volume small-print edition to be read with a magnifying glass is also available. Different from all other English-language dictionaries since it traces the history of each word as actually used during the last 800 years. The historical development of words is profusely illustrated with over 1,800,-000 quotations. Total vocabulary is over 400,000 words.

119. ———. ———. *A Supplement to the Oxford English Dictionary.* Ed. by R. W. Burchfield. Oxford: Clarendon Press, 1972-1978 Vol. 1, A-G. 1,331 pp.; Vol. 2, H-N, 1,282 pp. (In progress.)

To be completed in three volumes to replace the supplement of 1933. Will include words that have appeared in the English language both in Britain and elsewhere from 1884 to the present.

120. ———. *The Shorter Oxford English Dictionary on Historical Principles;* prepared by William Little, H. W. Fowler, and Jessie Coulson. Rev. and ed. by C. T. Onions. 3d ed., completely reset, with etymologies by G. W. S. Friedrichsen and

with revised addenda. Oxford: Clarendon Press, 1973. 2,672 pp.

The authorized abridgment of the *Oxford English Dictionary* (see no. 118).

ETYMOLOGICAL DICTIONARIES

121. *Oxford Dictionary of English Etymology.* C. T. Onions, ed. Oxford: Clarendon Press, 1966. 1,025 pp.

The standard scholarly work.

122. Klein, Ernest. *A Comprehensive Etymological Dictionary of the English Language.* Amsterdam: Elsevier Publishing Co., 1966–1967. 2 vols.

An amazing work of erudition by a Czech rabbi who emigrated to Canada after World War II. Contains more entries than the *Oxford Dictionary of English Etymology.*

SYNONYM AND ANTONYM DICTIONARIES

123. Hayakawa, Samuel Ichiyé, *et al. Funk & Wagnalls Modern Guide to Synonyms and Related Words.* New York: Funk & Wagnalls Company, Inc., 1968. 726 pp.

Contains highly readable textual essays.

124. Roget, Peter Mark. *The Original Roget's Thesaurus of English Words and Phrases.* New ed., completely revised and modernized by Robert A. Dutch. New York: St. Martin's Press, Inc., 1965. 1,405 pp.

First published 1852; arranged in classified order with an alphabetical word index. British orientation.

125. *Roget's International Thesaurus.* 4th ed. New York: Thomas Y. Crowell Company, 1977.

First published 1886; similar to the above work, but includes more American words, phrases, and colloquialisms.

126. *Webster's New Dictionary of Synonyms;* a dictionary of discriminated synonyms, with antonyms and analogous and contrasted words. 2d ed. G. & C. Merriam Company, 1968. 909 pp.

One of the most useful of this type of dictionary.

CHAPTER III

Bible

This chapter will be the longest of this work because there are more bibliographic and reference tools for Biblical studies than for any other area of theology. In fact, there are so many such tools that this chapter will present only those which deal with the whole Bible, while the next chapter will consider those which deal with a specific part of the Bible, such as the Old Testament or the New Testament.

GUIDES AND MANUALS

127. Danker, Frederick W. *Multipurpose Tools for Bible Study.* 3d ed. St. Louis: Concordia Publishing House, 1970. 295 pp.

A bibliographic essay by a Lutheran Biblical scholar who discusses in detail such tools as concordances, texts, grammars, lexicons, dictionaries, versions, and commentaries published up to 1968. Includes a most useful chapter on major commentary series published in the United States and abroad. Also discusses commentaries on the various books of the Bible. A basic tool for anyone engaged in serious Biblical study.

128. American Baptist Seminary of the West. Covina Campus. *The Tools of Biblical Interpretation; A Bibliographical Guide.* By faculty and students of the California Baptist Theological Seminary. Edited by James Hester and Genevieve Kelly. Covina, Calif., 1968. 133 pp.

————. ————. *1968–1970 Supplement.* Covina, Calif., 1970. 18 pp.

A series of bibliographic essays and bibliographies by various authors on basic Biblical tools.

129. Glanzman, George S., and Fitzmyer, Joseph A. *An Introductory Bibliography for the Study of Scripture.* Westminster, Md.: The Newman Press, 1961. 135 pp. (Woodstock Papers, Occasional Essays for Theology, No. 5.)

An annotated, selective bibliography of 342 tools compiled by two Catholic Biblical scholars. Includes both English and foreign-language works; ecumenical in orientation. Includes chapters on periodicals and series as well as on the other basic tools. Designed for Catholic seminarians.

130. Princeton Theological Seminary. Library. *A Bibliography of Bible Study for Theological Students.* Princeton: Princeton Theological Seminary, 1960. 107 pp.

An annotated, classified bibliography with strong emphasis on both Old Testament and New Testament commentaries.

131. Interpretation. *Tools for Bible Study.* Ed. by Balmer H. Kelly and Donald G. Miller. Richmond, Va.: John Knox Press, 1956. 159 pp.

Consists of eleven bibliographic essays by prominent Protestant Biblical scholars; appeared originally as a series of articles in *Interpretation,* 1947–1949. While many important new tools have appeared since that time, this work continues to have value not only for its discussion of the tools themselves but also for its illustrations of how these tools can best be used.

132. Marrow, Stanley B. *Basic Tools for Biblical Exegesis.* Rome: Biblical Institute Press, 1976. 91 pp.

Annotated bibliography of 215 tools in English and other languages for the Biblical researcher. Often lists citations where critical reviews of the works listed may be found. Index included.

BIBLIOGRAPHY OF BIBLE TEXTS AND VERSIONS

133. British and Foreign Bible Society. Library. *Historical Catalogue of the Printed Editions of Holy Scripture in the Library of the British and Foreign Bible Society.* Compiled by T. H. Darlow and H. F. Moule. London: Bible House, 1903–1911. 2 vols. in 4.

Contents: Vol. 1, English; Vol. 2, Polyglots and languages other than English arranged alphabetically by language.

"Under each language-heading, all editions—whether complete Bibles, Testaments, or separate portions—are arranged in strictly chronological order according to their dates of publication" (Preface). Indexes include: languages and dialects (over 600); translators, revisers, editors; printers, publishers; places of printing; general subjects. This is an important collection of over 10,000 volumes.

134. Herbert, Arthur Sumner. *Historical Catalogue of Printed Editions of the English Bible, 1525–1961;* revised and expanded from the edition of T. H. Darlow and H. F. Moule, 1903. London: British and Foreign Bible Society; New York: American Bible Society, 1968. 549 pp.

Based not only on the collection of the British and Foreign Bible Society in London but also on ten other British and American collections: the British Museum; the Bodleian; Cambridge University; National Library of Scotland; Trinity College, Dublin; Huntington Library; Newberry Library; Harvard; New York Public Library; and the American Bible Society. Indicates locations and provides some annotations. Arranged chronologically by date of publication. Includes indexes similar to Darlow and Moule (no. 133).

135. Hills, Margaret T., ed. *The English Bible in America;* a bibliography of editions of the Bible and the New Testament published in America, 1777–1957. New York: American Bible Society and New York Public Library, 1961. 477 pp.

Lists in chronological order, with annotations and locations, English-language Bibles published in the United States and Canada. Includes geographical index, index of publishers and printers, index of translations, translators and revisers, index of editors and commentators, index of edition titles, and general index.

RETROSPECTIVE BIBLIOGRAPHY

136. Jerusalem. École Biblique et Archéologique Française. Bibliothèque. *Catalogue de la Bibliothèque de l'École Biblique et Archéologique Française* (Catalog of the Library of the French Biblical and Archaeological School). Jerusalem, Israel; Boston: G. K. Hall & Co., 1975. 13 vols.

Photocopied reproduction in book form of the catalog of one of the world's outstanding Biblical collections. "Today the holdings of the library amount to over 55,000 volumes in all languages dealing with such topics as Old and New Testament, Judaism, Christian Antiquity, Papyrology, Linguistics, Epigraphy, Numismatics, Archaeology, Egyptology, Geography, Oriental History, Biblical Theology, etc. Since the École Biblique was deeply involved both in the excavation of Qumran and the official publication of the Dead Sea Scrolls, it acquired all the significant material on this subject" (Preface). Provides cataloging for both books and articles. Author and subject entries are integrated in a single alphabetical sequence. Entries under each subject are arranged chronologically. Entries for prolific authors list books first and then articles.

137. Langevin, Paul-Émile. *Bibliographie Biblique. Biblical Bibliography. Biblische Bibliographie. Bibliografía Biblica. Bibliografía Bíblica. 1930–1970.* Quebec: Les Presses de l'Université Laval, 1972. 935 pp.

A classified index of 70 Catholic periodicals and 286 Catholic books published 1930–1970. Main sections are introduction to the Bible, Old and New Testaments, Christ, Biblical themes. Includes author index, subject index, and table of contents in five languages.

INDEXES AND ABSTRACTS

138. *Elenchus Bibliographicus Biblicus.* Vol. 49 ff., 1968 to date. Rome: Biblical Institute Press. 1968 to date. Annual.

From 1920 to 1968 this was part of the journal *Biblica.* The *Elenchus* is the primary index for Biblical studies. While edited by a Catholic scholar, it is ecumenical and international in scope. Lists without annotations both journal articles and books in classified order. Provides author-subject index, index of words in Hebrew, Greek, and other languages. Students should not be put off by the Latin title or the Latin subject headings, which are easily translated and yield numerous works in English as well as other languages.

139. *Internationale Zeitschriftenschau für Bibelwissenschaft und Grenzgebiete. International Review of Biblical Studies.*

Revue Internationale des Études Bibliques, 1951/1952 to date. Düsseldorf: Patmos-Verlag, 1952 to date. Biennial.

Indexes approximately 400 periodicals as well as Festschriften, reports, and book reviews. Abstracts usually in German. Arranged in classified order. Provides author index. Excellent supplement to *Elenchus Bibliographicus Biblicus* (no. 138).

OLDER BIBLE DICTIONARIES AND ENCYCLOPEDIAS

140. Hastings, James. *Dictionary of the Bible,* dealing with its language, literature, and contents, including the Biblical theology. Edinburgh: T. & T. Clark; New York: Charles Scribner's Sons, 1898–1904. 5 vols.

A standard, older British work representing a more "moderate" position in the area of Biblical criticism than Cheyne (no. 141). Long, signed articles with bibliographies; intended for scholar, student, and general reader. Vol. 5 consists of additional articles and an index to the whole set.

141. Cheyne, Thomas Kelly, and Black, J. S. *Encyclopaedia Biblica;* a critical dictionary of the literary, political, and religious history, the archaeology, geography, and natural history of the Bible. New York: The Macmillan Company, 1899–1903. 4 vols.

Represents "advanced" Biblical criticism. Written for the scholar and the professional Bible student. This work is dedicated to Professor William Robertson Smith, who inspired its undertaking but died before he was able to begin the editing of it.

142. *International Standard Bible Encyclopaedia.* James Orr, general ed. Chicago: The Howard-Severance Company, 1915. 5 vols. (Reprint: Grand Rapids, Mich.: Wm. B. Eerdmans Publishing Company, 1960.)

"Its general attitude may be described as that of a reasonable conservatism" (Preface). Less "advanced" and less technical than Cheyne. Intended more for pastor and Bible student. Signed articles, some with bibliographies.

MORE RECENT BIBLE DICTIONARIES
AND ENCYCLOPEDIAS

143. *Catholic Biblical Encyclopedia,* by John E. Steinmueller
and Kathryn Sullivan. New York: Joseph F. Wagner, Inc.,
1956. 2 vols.

Contents: Old Testament, 1956. 1,163 pp.; New Testament,
1950. 679 pp.

This work is "the first Catholic Biblical encyclopedia in the
English language. . . . It was not written for Biblical specialists,
but for the great majority of educated people" (Introduction,
Vol. 1). Represents pre-Vatican II Catholic Biblical scholarship.

144. *The Interpreter's Dictionary of the Bible.* George Arthur
Buttrick, ed. New York and Nashville: Abingdon Press, 1962.
4 vols.

————. ————. *Supplementary Volume.* Keith Crim, ed.
Nashville: Abingdon Press, 1976. 998 pp.

The basic current, Protestant-oriented, multivolume Bible
dictionary, which fills the same need for this generation as Hastings (no. 140) did for a previous generation. Contributors to the
original four-volume work included 253 scholars from throughout the world, while 271 scholars of similar stature contributed
to the Supplement. The Supplement contains cross-references to
articles in the original work and current printings of the original
work carry cross-references to the Supplement. Articles are
signed and have bibliographies appended. For those who are
beginning research on a Biblical subject, the *IDB* provides an
excellent entry point for developing a bibliography of further
works to be consulted. All five volumes are designed for the
preacher, teacher, student, and general reader.

145. Douglas, James Dixon (and others). *The New Bible
Dictionary.* Grand Rapids, Mich.: Wm. B. Eerdmans Publishing Company, 1962. 1,375 pp.

This work is the "product of the Tyndale Fellowship for
Biblical Research, which was founded in 1945 in close association with the Inter-Varsity Fellowship to stimulate evangelical
biblical scholarship in Great Britain and elsewhere" (Preface).
Articles are initialed and often carry bibliographies. Useful for
laity as well as clergy.

146. Hastings, James. *Dictionary of the Bible.* Rev. ed. Edited by Frederick C. Grant and H. H. Rowley. New York: Charles Scribner's Sons, 1963. 1,059 pp.

The 1st ed. of 1909 was an entirely new work and not a condensation of Hastings' *Dictionary of the Bible,* 1898–1904, 5 vols. (no. 140).

In this new edition of the earlier one-volume work, "not everything has been rewritten, but every entry has been read by a competent scholar. Some entries have been passed as needing no change; some have been partly modified; some have been wholly rewritten . . . . There are many new entries, sometimes dealing with new sources of knowledge, such as the Dead Sea Scrolls, and sometimes with Biblical terms which were not included in the old edition" (Preface). A first-rate work representing a wide selection of prominent British and American Biblical scholars.

147. *Encyclopedic Dictionary of the Bible,* tr. by Louis F. Hartman. New York: McGraw-Hill Book Co., Inc., 1963. 2,634 pp.

Subtitle: A translation and adaptation of A. van den Born's *Bijbels Woordenboek,* 2d rev. ed., 1954–1957.

"Most of the longer articles, especially those of a theological nature, have been translated quite faithfully, with little or no changes made in them . . . . On the other hand, many of the shorter articles, particularly those concerned with philological, historical, or archaeological matters, have been largely rewritten in English, often for the sake of bringing them closer to what the English editor believes to be the best present-day opinions on these matters" (Foreword). English titles have been substituted for Dutch titles in the bibliographies. A more faithful French translation rather than adaptation of the original Dutch work is also available (*Dictionnaire Encyclopédique de la Bible,* Turnhout, 1960). Represents modern Catholic Biblical scholarship.

148. Cornfeld, Gaalyahu, ed. *Pictorial Biblical Encyclopedia;* a visual guide to the Old and New Testaments. New York: The Macmillan Company; London: Collier-Macmillan, Ltd., 1964. 712 pp.

The work of Jewish Biblical scholars. "The edifice of biblical thought is here considered as a whole, with the emphasis on a historical, rather than specifically theological approach" (Introduction). Popularly written, well illustrated with photographs; no bibliographies.

149. McKenzie, John L. *Dictionary of the Bible.* Milwaukee: Bruce Publishing Company, 1965. 954 pp.

Written by an outstanding American Catholic Biblical scholar for the general reader. No bibliographies appended to articles, but a bibliography at the beginning of the work, pp. xi-xiv; few cross-references.

150. Gehman, Henry Snyder. *The New Westminster Dictionary of the Bible.* Philadelphia: The Westminster Press, 1970. 1,127 pp.

A completely new work and not merely a revision of the *Westminster Dictionary of the Bible* (1944), which the author had previously revised from the *Davis Bible Dictionary* (1898–1924). An up-to-date, Protestant-oriented, attractively printed work with ample cross-references; no bibliography. New illustrations; maps from the *Westminster Historical Maps of Bible Lands* by G. E. Wright and F. V. Filson included. Useful for pastors, students, and lay Bible teachers.

151. Miller, Madeleine Sweeney, and Miller, J. Lane. *Harper's Bible Dictionary.* 8th ed. New York: Harper & Row, Publishers, Inc., 1973. 853 pp.

An extensively revised edition of a popular work first published in 1952. Based on solid scholarly research and consultation. Archaeological and theological articles especially have received extensive rewriting and updating. Intended for "the genuinely interested layman and the more seriously interested student and minister" (Foreword). Protestant in orientation.

DICTIONARIES OF BIBLICAL THEOLOGY

In the last generation there have appeared a number of Bible dictionaries that deal with the theology or the concepts presented in the Bible and exclude discussion of persons, places, customs, manners, rites, and rituals unless these have obvious and important theological significance. The most comprehensive of such dictionaries is the German work edited by Gerhard

Kittel and now translated into English in its entirety under the title *Theological Dictionary of the New Testament* (no. 287). While the title indicates that it deals with the words of the New Testament, it does include extensive material on the Old Testament as it traces New Testament words and concepts back through their Old Testament and also Hellenistic roots.

Listed here are four works indicative of the international and ecumenical scope of Biblical studies. One work is British, another Swiss, another German, and the fourth French in origin. Two represent primarily Protestant scholarship and two represent primarily Catholic scholarship. All are works that will prove most useful to the pastor, teacher, student, and scholar.

152. Richardson, Alan. *A Theological Word Book of the Bible.* London: SCM Press, Ltd., 1950. 290 pp.

Clear, concise, signed articles, often with bibliographies, by thirty-one British Protestant scholars. "Broadly, it may be said that, while accepting 'ex anima' the methods of scientific criticism, the common point of view is that the key to the biblical revelation is Christ, who is the proper subject both of the Old and the New Testaments" (Preface). A useful tool for Biblical preaching and teaching.

153. Allmen, Jean-Jacques von, ed. *A Companion to the Bible.* New York: Oxford University Press, 1958. 479 pp.

Translated from the 2d French ed., 1956. The work of some thirty-seven Swiss and French Protestant scholars; designed for the general reader as well as the minister. Consists of fewer articles, sometimes several columns long, rather than many short articles. Aims at being "a popular manual of biblical theology, the principal ideas of which are classified alphabetically." Evangelical in tone.

154. Bauer, Johannes B., ed. *Sacramentum Verbi; An Encyclopedia of Biblical Theology.* New York: Herder & Herder, Inc., 1970. 3 vols.

Translated from the 3d enlarged and revised German edition of 1967, a work produced by European Catholic scholars. Long signed articles with the same bibliography that appeared in the German edition plus some additional English-language works or translations. Combines both the academic and the pastoral concerns. Vol. 3 contains supplemental bibliography, analytical index of articles and cross-references, index of Biblical references, and index of Hebrew and Greek words. "Represents one of the finest fruits of the renewal in Roman Catholic biblical scholarship" (Foreword to the English Edition).

155. Leon-Dufour, Xavier, ed. *Dictionary of Biblical Theology.* 2d ed., rev. and enl. New York: The Seabury Press, Inc., 1973. 712 pp.

Translated from the French rev. ed., 1968. The work of some seventy French-speaking Catholic scholars who attempt to serve both scientific and pastoral needs. Most articles include numerous cross-references. No bibliography. Provides an analytic table listing subject headings and cross-references, and a classified index of topics. A most useful tool for both clergy and laity.

DICTIONARIES OF BIBLE LIFE, MANNERS, AND CUSTOMS

156. Miller, Madeleine Sweeney, and Miller, J. Lane. *Encyclopedia of Bible Life.* Rev. ed. London: A. & C. Black, Ltd., 1957. 493 pp.

First published by Harper in 1944, rev. ed., 1955. First British ed., 1957. Consists of twenty-two sections arranged in alphabetical order from "agriculture," "animals," through "water supply," "worship." Numerous photographs. Includes index of Biblical quotations and general index. The authors seek "to make a significant contribution to visual biblical education by presenting to teachers, ministers and students a compact source book of fully illustrated information bearing upon the people whose faith and habits and skills produced the Scriptures" (Preface).

157. Corswant, W. *A Dictionary of Life in Bible Times.* New York: Oxford University Press, 1960. 308 pp.

Translated from the French ed., 1956. A popularly written work intended for students, teachers, and clergy. Includes numerous line drawings, a systematic classification of principal articles, and an alphabetical index of contents. Based upon scholarly research. Excludes treatment of political history, geography, and theological or literary questions.

DICTIONARY OF BIBLICAL ARCHAEOLOGY

158. Pfeiffer, Charles F., ed. *The Biblical World: A Dictionary of Biblical Archaeology.* Grand Rapids, Mich.: Baker Book House, 1966. 612 pp.

Popularly written, generally short articles, often with bibliographies. Numerous photographs. "Biblical persons and places are mentioned only if archaeology has added to our knowledge of them. Major archaeological terms are defined to help the reader with no professional training in the subject to get the most out of the many valuable archaeological books that are now available" (Introduction).

HISTORY OF THE BIBLE

159. *The Cambridge History of the Bible.* Cambridge: University Press, 1963–1970. 3 vols.

Contents: Vol. 1, *From the Beginnings to Jerome,* ed. by P. R. Ackroyd and C. F. Evans, 1970, 649 pp.; Vol. 2, *The West from the Fathers to the Reformation,* ed. by G. W. H. Lampe, 1969, 566 pp.; Vol. 3, *The West from the Reformation to the Present Day,* ed. by S. L. Greenslade, 1963, 590 pp.

A work of erudition by an international and ecumenical group of scholars. Covers the development of the Bible in ancient, medieval, and modern world. Includes discussion of such topics as languages, text, canon, exegesis, versions, commentaries, criticism, and influence of the Bible throughout its history. Bibliography, general index, and Bible reference index are included at the end of each volume.

ENGLISH VERSIONS AND TRANSLATIONS

Listed in this section are some of the English versions and translations still in use today, with brief annotations for each entry. A distinction is made here between a version and a translation. A version represents the work of a group of scholars who have in some manner been appointed or approved by several Protestant churches, by a council of churches, by the Catholic Church or one of its orders or a major geographical area. A translation, on the other hand, represents the work of one or several individuals who more or less "privately" undertake to render the Bible into English. Such translations will often be freer renderings or even paraphrasings of the original texts and will tend to serve more for study purposes than for liturgical use in the churches.

More detailed studies on versions and translations may be found in *The Cambridge History of the Bible* (no. 159), Vol. 3, pp. 141–174, 361–382; F. F. Bruce, *The History of the Bible in English,* 3d ed. (New York: Oxford University Press, 1978); Geddes MacGregor, *A Literary History of the Bible; From the Middle Ages to the Present Day* (Nashville: Abingdon Press, 1968); and Herbert May, *Our English Bible in the Making,* rev. ed. (Philadelphia: The Westminster Press, 1965). A brief discussion is also included in Edward Blair, *Abingdon Bible Handbook* (no. 217), pp. 38–56.

PROTESTANT VERSIONS

160. *King James Version* or *Authorized Version,* 1611.

The most influential of all English versions. Still widely used among Protestants. English professors often have more attachment to it than theologians because its literary quality, like Shakespeare's, endures, although much of its language has now become archaic.

161. *Revised Version,* 1881–1885.

The work of British scholars who attempted to update the King James Version. The New Testament was published in 1881 and the Old Testament in 1885. The suggestions for revision made by the American members of the committee were largely unacceptable to their British counterparts. Hence the American Standard Version (no. 162) was later published in the United States.

162. *American Standard Version.* New York: Thomas Nelson & Sons, 1901.

The American edition of the Revised Version (no. 161). Still a useful version for study purposes, as it is quite literal rather than literary in tone. Moreover, the editors arranged verses in paragraphs to help convey meaning and thought patterns more clearly. Poetry in the Psalms, Proverbs, and elsewhere is printed in verse form rather than in paragraphs as prose. It is more accurate than the King James Version because it is based on more authoritative Biblical manuscripts discovered since 1611 and also benefits from a more advanced knowledge of the original languages.

163. *New American Standard Bible.* Chicago: Moody Press, 1971.

As the American Standard Version, 1901, was falling into disuse because of age and because of the appearance of many newer versions and translations, the Lockman Foundation of La Habra, California, provided the funding for an updating and revising of the ASV. Marginal cross-references were added, but the paragraphing of the ASV was replaced by a verse-by-verse format. Has special appeal for more conservative Protestants.

164. *Revised Standard Version.* New York: Thomas Nelson & Sons, 1952.

The New Testament was issued first in 1946 and the whole Bible in 1952. Based on the King James Version (1611), and the American Standard Version (1901). "The Revised Standard Version is not a new translation in the language of today. It is not a paraphrase which aims at striking idioms. It is a revision which seeks to preserve all that is best in the English Bible as it has been known and used through the years. It is intended for use in public and private worship, not merely for reading and instruction" (Preface). In 1957 an RSV of the Apocrypha was also published. The whole work, known as *The Common Bible,* has now been approved by the Roman Catholic and Orthodox Churches also. While some still feel strongly opposed to it, the RSV is probably the most widely used of English versions in the world today.

165. *The New English Bible with the Apocrypha.* Oxford: University Press; and Cambridge: University Press, 1970.

New Testament published, 1961; Old Testament and Apocrypha, 1970. Planned and directed by the Church of Scotland, the Church of England, the English Methodist, Congregational, and Presbyterian Churches, the Society of Friends, Councils of Churches, and Bible Societies as an entirely new translation based upon the best Greek and Hebrew texts, and not as a revision of the King James Version. It is intended for both worship and study purposes. While the language is dignified, clear, and accurate, American readers will find some Briticisms.

166. *New International Version.* Grand Rapids, Mich.: Zondervan Publishing House.

New Testament, 1973; Old Testament, not yet issued, but expected shortly. Produced by over one hundred conservative, evangelical scholars under the sponsorship of the New York Bible Society International. It is an entirely new version and not a revision of an older version. Intended for those who find the Revised Standard Version and *The New English Bible* (nos. 164, 165) too "liberal" and the one-person paraphrases too "idiosyncratic." It is concerned with both accuracy of translation and felicity in English style. It is arranged in paragraph form with captions at the beginning of sections.

CATHOLIC VERSIONS

167. *Douay-Rheims-Challoner Version,* 1582–1763.

The New Testament was published in Rheims, 1582, and the Old Testament in Douay, 1609–10. Both were extensively revised by Bishop Challoner of London from 1749 through 1763. This has been the standard translation for English-speaking Catholics up until the middle of the twentieth century. This version is based on the Latin Vulgate rather than on the Hebrew and Greek originals.

168. *Confraternity Version.* Paterson, N.J.: St. Anthony Guild Press, 1941–1961.

The Episcopal Committee of the Confraternity of Christian Doctrine appointed a committee of American Catholic scholars to revise the Challoner-Rheims New Testament. This revision, based on the Latin Vulgate but with consultation of the Greek text, was published in 1941. A new translation of the Old Testament was also sponsored by the Confraternity of Christian Doctrine. This work, based on the Hebrew text rather than the Vulgate, began publication in 1948 and was completed in four volumes in 1961.

169. *The Jerusalem Bible.* Garden City, N.Y.: Doubleday & Company, Inc., 1966. 1,547 pp., 498 pp.

Includes a new translation by Catholic scholars from the original Hebrew and Greek texts with English translation of the introductions and notes that appeared in the French edition, 1956, produced by the Dominican Biblical School in Jerusalem. A chronological table, an index of Biblical themes, and maps are appended. A most useful study tool.

170. *The New American Bible.* New York and Beverly Hills, Calif.: Benziger Brothers, 1970. 1,347 pp., 401 pp.

Includes a revision of the *Confraternity Version* of the Old Testament (no. 168), plus a completely new translation of the New Testament based on the Greek text rather than the Vulgate. Produced by members of the Catholic Biblical Association of America, including four Protestant scholars, sponsored by the Bishops' Committee of the Confraternity of Christian Doctrine. Intended for liturgical use, private reading, and the purposes of students. Arranged in paragraph form with captions at the beginning of sections; extensive footnotes. Poetry is printed in verse form. Includes brief introductions to each book of the Bible, a glossary of Biblical theology terms, a survey of Biblical geography, and maps. Spelling of proper names "follows the customary forms found in most English Bibles since the Authorized Version" (Preface). Useful for both Catholics and Protestants.

JEWISH VERSIONS

171. *Jewish Version,* 1917. *The Holy Scriptures According to the Masoretic Text: A New Translation.* Philadelphia: The Jewish Publication Society of America, 1917.

A Jewish revision of what Christians call the "Old Testament" of the Revised Version, 1885 (no. 161). Since 1955 a completely new Jewish version has been in process.

PRIVATE TRANSLATIONS

172. Moffatt, James. *A New Translation of the Bible.* New York: Harper & Brothers, 1935. 1,039 pp., 329 pp.

One of the most popular and most brilliant of the one-person translations. The New Testament was published in 1913, the

Old Testament, 1924. Both were brought together in 1928 and appeared in a final revised form in 1935. Moffatt, a Scot, sometimes injects Scottish idioms, takes liberties in rearranging the text, and attempts to indicate the various sources of the Pentateuch by different type styles. His use of "the Eternal" for the name of God has never received acceptance. He served as executive secretary of the Revised Standard Version (no. 164) committee from 1937 until his death in 1944.

173. Smith, J. M. Powis, and Goodspeed, Edgar J. *The Complete Bible; An American Translation.* Chicago: The University of Chicago Press, 1939.

The Old Testament is the work of T. J. Meek, Leroy Waterman, A. R. Gordon, and J. M. P. Smith, while the New Testament and Apocrypha are the work of Edgar J. Goodspeed. Both Testaments are in simple, direct American English.

174. *The Bible in Basic English.* New York: E. P. Dutton & Co., Inc., 1950.

Produced by a committee of scholars in England under the direction of S. H. Hooke of the University of London. A straightforward, direct translation using only a one-thousand-word vocabulary. Would be especially useful for anyone just learning English as a second language.

175. Knox, Ronald A. *The Holy Bible;* a translation from the Latin Vulgate in the light of the Hebrew and Greek originals; authorized by the Hierarchy of England and Wales and the Hierarchy of Scotland. New York: Sheed & Ward, Inc., 1955.

A highly literate and understandable translation by an English Catholic. The New Testament appeared in 1944 and the Old Testament in two volumes in 1948 and 1950. The single volume containing the complete Bible appeared in 1955. Numerous footnotes.

176. Lamsa, George M. *The Holy Bible from Ancient Eastern Manuscripts: Containing the Old and New Testaments Translated from the Peshitta, The Authorized Bible of the Church of the East.* Philadelphia: A. J. Holman Company, 1957.

A translation from the Syriac version of the Hebrew Old Testament and the Greek New Testament known as the "Peshitta" (Simple). Lamsa's claim that the Peshitta gives more direct access to the Biblical texts, thought, and world view than do the Greek and Hebrew has not been accepted by the scholarly community.

177. Verkuyl, Gerrit (and others). *The New Berkeley Version in Modern English.* Grand Rapids, Mich.: Zondervan Publishing House, 1970.

A private, conservative counterpart to the Revised Standard Version. Verkuyl, a Presbyterian, translated the New Testament, which was first published in 1945, and supervised a group of conservative Old Testament scholars in the translation of the Old Testament, which was published in 1959. After Verkuyl's death, the publishers appointed several New Testament scholars to revise the New Testament. The resulting work was *The New Berkeley Version,* 1970. Includes brief footnotes and dates, reflecting conservative views.

178. Siewart, Francis E. *The Amplified Bible.* Grand Rapids, Mich.: Zondervan Publishing House, 1965.

Published in parts from 1954 until the whole Bible was published in 1965. Attempts to amplify key words or phrases by adding one or many synonyms set apart by parentheses or dashes. Adds commentary by supplying additional words in brackets or providing footnotes. Adopts a conservative viewpoint throughout.

179. *Good News Bible; The Bible in Today's English Version.* New York: American Bible Society, 1976.

Begun in 1964 with the Gospel of Mark, the New Testament was completed in 1966, with rev. eds. in 1971 and 1976. The whole Bible was published in 1976. An extremely popular, inexpensive translation using contemporary American English; intended both for those who speak English as their mother tongue and for those who speak it as an acquired language. Includes a word list that explains technical terms and rarely used words, has a listing of New Testament passages from the Septuagint, maps and map index, chronology of the Bible, and subject index. Numerous striking stylized line drawings illustrate the text. Especially useful for youth or lay Bible study as well as for private reading.

180. Taylor, Kenneth Nathaniel. *The Living Bible, Paraphrased.* Wheaton, Ill.: Tyndale House Publishers; London: Coverdale House Publishers, Ltd., 1971.

Began appearing with *Living Letters,* 1962, and was completed with the whole Bible in 1971. A popular, conservatively oriented paraphrase rather than a word-for-word translation. The translator acknowledges that "when the Greek or Hebrew is not clear, then the theology of the translator is his guide. . . . The theological lodestar in this book has been a rigid evangelical position" (Preface). Must be used with other translations or with the original Greek and Hebrew texts to determine what is Bible and what is commentary on the Bible.

For translations of the New Testament only, see nos. 270–278.

CONCORDANCES TO ENGLISH VERSIONS AND TRANSLATIONS

181. Cruden, Alexander. *Complete Concordance to the Old and New Testament . . . with . . . a Concordance to the Apocrypha* . . . London: Warne, 1737. 719 pp.

Published in many revised and enlarged editions by various publishers. Includes three parts: a concordance to the Old and New Testaments; a table of the proper names and their meanings; and a concordance to the Apocrypha. This work, which is not "complete," is now largely superseded except for its concordance to the Apocrypha. The latter is not reprinted in the more recent editions.

182. Young, Robert. *Analytical Concordance to the Bible,* . . . containing about 311,000 references, subdivided under the Hebrew and Greek originals, with the literal meaning and pronunciation of each. . . . Also index lexicons to the Old and New Testaments . . . and a complete list of Scripture proper names. 22d American ed., rev. by W. B. Stevenson. New York: Funk & Wagnalls, 1955. 1,090; 93; 23; and 51 pp. (Reprint: Grand Rapids, Mich.: Wm. B. Eerdmans Publishing Company, 1972.)

1st ed., 1879; rev. in 1902 by William B. Stevenson. Later editions, with few changes, are reprints of the 1902 edition, plus a supplement, 1936, entitled "Recent Discoveries in Bible Lands" by William F. Albright.

Listing under the English word the Hebrew and Greek originals, and then citing locations, makes this work more sophisticated than Cruden's. For a new analytical concordance of the Revised Standard Version New Testament, see Morrison (no. 269).

183. Strong, James. *The Exhaustive Concordance of the Bible.* London: Hodder; New York: Hunt, 1894 (copr. 1890). 1,340; 262; 126; and 79 pp.

Often reprinted (New York and Nashville: Abingdon Press, 1958). Includes the main concordance; a comparative concordance of the Authorized and Revised versions, including the American variations; a concise dictionary of the words in the Hebrew Bible; a concise dictionary of the words in the Greek Testament. The most complete concordance of the King James (Authorized) Version.

184. Hazard, Marshall Custis. *A Complete Concordance to the American Standard Version of the Holy Bible.* New York: Thomas Nelson & Sons, 1922. 1,234 pp.

Omits prepositions, auxiliaries, and other unimportant words; contains about 300,000 references arranged under 1,600 headings and subheadings.

185. Ellison, John W. *Nelson's Complete Concordance of the Revised Standard Version Bible.* Comp. under the supervision of John W. Ellison. New York: Thomas Nelson & Sons, 1957. 2,157 pp.

Attempts to be "complete" although not "exhaustive," as it omits over 130 frequently used words (e.g.: a, about, above, . . . you, your, yours), which account for approximately 59 percent of the text of the Bible. Because it was computer-produced, it cannot be "analytical." It gives the context and location of each and every word listed, but not the Hebrew or Greek words from which they were translated.

186. Metzger, Bruce M., and Metzger, Isobel M. *The Oxford Concise Concordance to the Revised Standard Version of the Holy Bible.* New York: Oxford University Press, 1962. 158 pp.

Prepared for the general reader; includes the more significant words and contexts. Proper names are placed in the main alphabetical sequence rather than in a separate list. Brief bibliographic or geographical information often included.

187. Thompson, Newton Wayland, and Stock, Raymond. *Complete Concordance to the Bible (Douay Version).* St. Louis

and London: B. Herder Book Company, 1945. 1,914 pp.

Revised and enlarged from the 1st ed. of 1942.

188. Gant, William John. *The Moffatt Bible Concordance; A Complete Concordance to: The Bible, A New Translation by James Moffatt.* New York: Harper & Brothers, 1950. 550 pp.

The British edition was published under the title *Concordance of the Bible in the Moffatt Translation* (London: Hodder & Stoughton, Ltd., 1950). "The *Concordance* is made up of between 60,000 and 70,000 references, each verse in the *New Translation* being, therefore, listed under from two to three separate words" (Introduction).

189. Speer, Jack Atkeson. *The Living Bible Concordance,* complete. Poolesville, Md., Poolesville Presbyterian Church, 1973. 1,209 pp.

A computer-produced complete concordance of Taylor's *The Living Bible, Paraphrased* (no. 180). The work of a group of volunteers in a small congregation.

190. *The Zondervan Expanded Concordance.* Grand Rapids, Mich.: Zondervan Publishing House, 1968. 1,848 pp.

Includes key words from the King James Version, the *Amplified Bible,* the *New Berkeley Version in Modern English,* the American Standard Version, *The New English Bible,* Phillips, and the Revised Standard Version, and the new words from the *New Scofield Bible.*

TOPICAL CONCORDANCES

191. Joy, Charles R. *Harper's Topical Concordance.* Rev. and enl. ed. New York: Harper & Row, Publishers, Inc., 1962. 628 pp.

1st ed., 1940.

Includes 33,200 Bible texts listed topically. "The present work will help one to find appropriate texts for a topic, even though the topic itself is not among the words of the text" (Preface).

192. *The New World Idea Index to the Holy Bible.* Harvey K. Griffith, ed. New York: The World Publishing Company, 1972. 907 pp.

"All texts are classified according to a predefined set of ideas rather than the actual words contained in the text." An elaborate system of concept relationship is worked out through numerous subheadings under each entry.

COMMENTARY SERIES

Listed in this section in chronological order from the date of the beginning of publication is a selection of twentieth-century commentary series on the whole Bible. These commentaries seem to divide themselves into the longer, more critical, exegetical, scholarly, and historical works on the one hand, and the shorter, more popular, homiletical and devotional works on the other. While the latter may be based on sound scholarship, they are intended more for the general reader than for the "serious student." Although the distinction between these two types of commentaries cannot be made hard and fast, it nevertheless serves a useful purpose in helping the reader make preliminary choices in a vast and often bewildering body of literature.

No attempt will be made here to evaluate any individual work within a commentary series. Needless to say, one volume can differ remarkably from another in the same series. Consulting more specialized bibliographies (nos. 127–132, 226) and actually dipping into the work itself are the best methods for determining which particular commentary suits the reader's unique need. Of course, many commentaries are published separately and not as part of a series. Such works, many of which are of high quality, are not cited here.

While libraries usually classify the individual volumes of a series separately rather than as a set, the reader can find all the library's holdings in a particular series listed together in the public card catalog under the title of the series.

Unless stated otherwise, the commentaries here listed are Protestant in orientation.

LONGER, MORE TECHNICAL COMMENTARIES

193. *International Critical Commentary on the Holy Scriptures of the Old and New Testaments.* Samuel Rolles Driver, Alfred Plummer, Charles Augustus Briggs, eds. Edinburgh: T.

& T. Clark; New York: Charles Scribner's Sons, 1895 ff.

Although the series is still incomplete, some forty volumes have appeared from Driver's *Deuteronomy* in 1895 until Montgomery's *Kings* in 1951. Comparable to the highest standards of German Biblical scholarship, this series by British and American Protestant scholars deals with the exegetical, philological, historical, and textual, but excludes the homiletical. While the *ICC* is uneven in quality and somewhat outdated, certain volumes continue to be extremely useful to both preacher and scholar, e.g., Driver, *Deuteronomy;* Moore, *Judges;* Sanday and Headlam, *Romans;* Burton, *Galatians;* Plummer, *St. Luke.*

194. *The Interpreter's Bible;* the Holy Scriptures in the King James and Revised Standard versions with general articles and introduction, exegesis, exposition for each book of the Bible. George A. Buttrick, ed. New York and Nashville: Abingdon Press, 1952–1957. 12 vols.

Aims to be both exegetical and expository. Produced by over 125 Protestant scholars and preachers from the English-speaking world. The King James and Revised Standard versions are printed in parallel columns at the top of each page, with the exegesis immediately below across the page, and the exposition below the exegesis in double columns. Each book of the Bible is preceded by an introduction. Generally the introductions, exegesis, and articles are the stronger parts of the work. The didactic and illustrative material in the exposition sections often tends to become verbose, superficial, and dated.

195. *The Anchor Bible.* William Foxwell Albright and David Noel Freedman, eds. Garden City, N.Y.: Doubleday & Company, Inc., 1964 ff.

A scholarly series with each work consisting of an introduction, a new translation, and extended commentary. Contributors are from many countries and represent Protestant, Catholic, and Jewish backgrounds. This work is aimed "at the general reader with no special formal training in biblical studies; yet, it is written with the most exacting standards of scholarship, reflecting the highest technical accomplishment" (General Editors). However, the volumes have tended to become so long that "the general reader" may become weary. The volume on Ephesians 1–3, for instance, extends 420 pages. On the other hand, student and specialist will appreciate the thoroughness.

196. *Hermeneia;* a critical and historical commentary on the Bible. Philadelphia: Fortress Press, 1971 ff.

Continues the *International Critical Commentary* tradition of critical and historical scholarship. Utilizes "the full range of philological and historical tools including textual criticism (often ignored in modern commentaries), the methods of the history of tradition (including genre and prosodic analysis), and the history of religion" (Foreword). Some volumes are English translations of recent commentaries already written in other languages. Contributors are international and interconfessional. This series is definitely designed for the serious student and scholar. It "eschews for itself homiletical translation of the Bible" (Foreword).

SHORTER, MORE POPULAR COMMENTARIES

197. *The Cambridge Bible for Schools and Colleges.* Cambridge: University Press, 1877–1925. 56 vols.

Though small volumes, the works in this series have had wide popularity. Based upon sound scholarship, they are designed for the general reader. Frequent revisions and completeness have further enhanced their usefulness.

198. *The Cambridge Bible Commentary; New English Bible.* P. C. Ackroyd, A. R. C. Leaney, J. W. Parker, gen. eds. Cambridge: University Press, 1963 ff.

A completely new series that assumes no specialized theological knowledge or acquaintance with Greek or Hebrew on the part of the reader. The results of modern Biblical scholarship are presented through brief introductions and comments on the text of *The New English Bible.* Each volume, approximately 200 pages in length, can be read consecutively from first to last page. The New Testament part of the series was completed in 1967. The Old Testament and Apocrypha sections are in progress.

199. *The New-Century Bible.* W. F. Adeney, gen. ed. New York: Frowde; Edinburgh: Jack, 1901–1922. 34 vols.

Small, pocket-size volumes intended for the general reader without knowledge of the Greek or Hebrew. Revised Version,

1881–1885, printed above with comments below on each page.

200. *New Century Bible;* based on the Revised Standard Version. Ronald E. Clements and Matthew Black, gen. eds. London: Oliphants, Ltd., 1967 ff. (In progress.)

An entirely new series with both British and American contributors. The Biblical text is omitted; thus, the comments are somewhat longer than in the older series. Attempts to bring the results of current scholarship to the general reader.

201. *Expositor's Bible.* W. Robertson Nicoll, ed. New York: Armstrong, 1902–1908. 49 vols. in 25.

Originally published 1887–1896. Didactic and homiletical rather than exegetical or critical. Volumes by outstanding authors of a former generation such as Marcus Dods, Alexander Maclaren, George Adam Smith, H. C. G. Moule, James Denney, Alfred Plummer, and William Milligan make this a series that is still on many preachers' shelves.

202. *The Clarendon Bible.* Oxford: Clarendon Press, 1922–1936. "It is not the writers' intention to set out the latest notions of radical scholars—English or foreign—nor even to describe the exact position at which the discussion of the various problems has arrived. The aim of the series is rather to put forward a constructive view of the books and their teaching, taking into consideration and welcoming results as to which there is a large measure of agreement among scholars" (Preface). Comments and notes based on the Revised Version, 1881–1885. Intended for use of students, clergy, and informed laity.

203. *The New Clarendon Bible.* Oxford: Clarendon Press, 1963 ff. (In progress.)

Intended to fill in the gaps of the old series (no. 202) and update it. The plan and form of the new series is essentially the same, except when the text is printed, it appears on the same page as the comments. The new series began using *The New English Bible* as its text, but later switched to the Revised Standard Version.

204. *Torch Bible Commentaries.* John Marsh, David M. Paton, Alan Richardson, gen. eds. London: SCM Press, Ltd.; Naperville, Ill.: Alec R. Allenson, Inc., 1949 ff. (In progress.)

Intended for the general reader. "The findings and views of modern critical scholarship on the text of the Bible have been taken fully into account. . . . But minute points of scholarship, of language or archaeology or text, have not been pushed into the foreground. We have asked the writers of the various books to have in mind the view that the Bible is more than a quarry for the practice of erudition; that it contains the living message of the living God" (Foreword to Series).

205. *The Layman's Bible Commentary.* Balmer H. Kelly, ed. Richmond, Va.: John Knox Press, 1959–1962. 25 vols.

Brief, nontechnical guides by competent scholars to help the layperson in personal study of the Bible. Based on the Revised Standard Version.

ONE-VOLUME COMMENTARIES ON THE WHOLE BIBLE

A one-volume commentary on the whole Bible obviously cannot give the detailed discussion of a passage, a phrase, or a word that is often required. And yet as a ready reference tool for quick, concise answers to particular questions, a one-volume commentary can often provide the information required. Moreover, introductory articles to the Bible as a whole as well as to individual books of the Bible enhance the value of this type of work. Evaluation of one-volume commentaries can be made by such standards as date of publication, number, and authority of the contributors and reputation of the publisher. Listed below in chronological order by date of publication are some of the better known twentieth-century works. All are from a Protestant orientation unless otherwise noted.

206. Dummelow, J. R., ed. *A Commentary on the Holy Bible,* by various writers. London: Macmillan & Co., Ltd., 1909. 1,092 pp.

Based on the King James Version and intended for the general reader.

207. Gore, Charles; Goudge, Henry Leighton; and Guillaume, Alfred. *A New Commentary on Holy Scripture,* including the Apocrypha. New York: The Macmillan Company, 1928. 697; 158; and 743 pp.

Represents the work of Anglican scholars who use the methods of Biblical criticism while holding to "the Catholic faith."

Especially valuable for its commentary on the Apocrypha, which is omitted in many other such works.

208. Eiselen, Frederick Carl; Lewis, Edwin; and Downey, David G., eds. *The Abingdon Bible Commentary.* New York: The Abingdon Press, Inc., 1929. 1,398 pp.

Uses "biblical scholarship for practical and evangelical purposes" (Foreword). Contributors include leading Biblical scholars of the English-speaking world from Methodist and other free-church traditions. Intended for pastors, church school teachers, and "intelligent laymen."

209. Clarke, W. K. Lowther. *Concise Bible Commentary.* New York: The Macmillan Company, 1953. 996 pp.

The work of one author, an Anglican clergyman who served as secretary of the S.P.C.K. Approximately one third of the work consists of background articles (pp. 1–333). Notes on the text are short and concise.

210. Orchard, Bernard, gen. ed. (and others). *A Catholic Commentary on Holy Scripture.* London: Thomas Nelson & Sons, Ltd., 1953. 1,312 pp. (For rev. ed., see no. 214.)

Produced by leading Catholic scholars from the English-speaking world; based on the Douay Version. Maintains loyalty to the Catholic faith while taking full cognizance of current Biblical criticism. Includes encyclopedic articles with bibliographies. Endeavors to "sum up the results of international scholarship during the last fifty years, and put them at the disposal not only of Catholics, but also of all those who respect and would be glad to know more of the Catholic Church's teaching on Scripture and of the way in which her members interpret it" (Preface).

211. Black, Matthew, gen. ed. and New Testament ed.; and Rowley, H. H., Old Testament ed. *Peake's Commentary on the Bible.* London: Thomas Nelson & Sons, Ltd., 1962. 1,126 pp.

1st ed., Arthur S. Peake, gen. ed., A. J. Grieve, asst. ed., 1919; Reprinted with Supplement by A. J. Grieve, 1937.

Both the original edition and the new work are best described by Peake's statement in the original: "The present work is designed to put before the reader in a simple form, without technicalities, the generally accepted results of Biblical Criticism, Interpretation, History and Theology. It is not intended to be homiletic or devotional, but to convey with precision, and yet in a popular and interesting way, the meaning of the original writers, and reconstruct the conditions in which they worked and of which they wrote. It will thus, while not explicitly devotional or practical, provide that accurate interpretation of the text through which alone the sound basis for devotional use and practical application can be laid" (Preface).

The 1962 edition, an entirely new work produced by leading scholars throughout the English-speaking world, maintains the same high standards of scholarship set by the earlier edition. Contains extensive general articles, introductory articles to the Old and New Testaments, each with bibliography, as well as commentaries on the Old and New Testaments based on the text of the Revised Standard Version. Also provides detailed index and maps revised and adapted from the Nelson *Atlas of the Bible.* Intended for laypersons, students, and clergy.

212. Pfeiffer, Charles F., Old Testament ed.; and Harrison, Everett F., New Testament ed. *The Wycliffe Bible Commentary.* Chicago: Moody Press, 1962. 1,525 pp.

Conservative Protestant orientation; based on the King James Version.

213. Brown, Raymond E.; Fitzmyer, Joseph A.; Murphy, Roland E. *The Jerome Biblical Commentary.* Englewood Cliffs, N.J.: Prentice-Hall, Inc., 1968. 637 and 889 pp.

This work, by some fifty contributors teaching in Catholic colleges and seminaries in North America and abroad, contains eighty articles, topical and commentary, covering the whole Bible, including the Apocrypha. All the contributors use to varying degrees the principles of modern Biblical criticism. Bibliographies listing Catholic and Protestant works in many languages are provided with each article as well as a bibliography of basic reference works at the end of Vol. 2. Comments are based on the original Hebrew, Aramaic, and Greek texts and not on the Vulgate or on any single English version. However, knowledge of the original languages is not necessary for using the commentary, which is intended for students, scholars, clergy, and laity.

The editors decided they could make the greatest contribution to ecumenicity by using only Catholic contributors. The

variation in interpretation among these representative scholars
"should destroy once and for all the myth of *the* Catholic position, as if there were a series of biblical interpretations or positions that all must profess. We hope that our non-Catholic
brethren can find in this commentary the same scientific method
and love for objectivity that characterize the best commentaries
written by scholars of their own denomination" (Editors' Preface). An extensive index is provided.

214. Fuller, Reginald C.; Johnston, Leonard; and Kearns,
Conleth. *A New Catholic Commentary on Holy Scripture.* New
and fully rev. ed. London: Thomas Nelson & Sons, Ltd., 1969.
1,377 pp.

1st ed., 1953 (no. 210).

The 1969 edition retains only one fifth of the material from
the earlier edition, but it keeps to the same aim of unfolding "the
genuine sense of the Scriptures while making the fullest use of
modern Biblical research. In the years since the appearance of
the first edition, Roman Catholic participation in Biblical study
has steadily grown and, in interpreting the Bible, the differences
between them and other denominations have diminished in
number and significance. . . . The word 'Catholic' has been
retained in the title of this commentary, not to indicate the
differences, such as they are, but to emphasize that this work is
a contribution by Roman Catholic scholars to the spread of
knowledge of the Word of God" (Preface).

The commentary is based on the original texts and contributors were free to make use of any English version they wished,
although the Revised Standard Version is given prominence.
Commentary is paragraph by paragraph rather than verse by
verse, with lengthy treatment of particular points given in the
introductory articles, which also contain updated bibliographies. Extensive index and updated maps are appended.

215. Guthrie, D., and Motyer, J. A., eds. *The New Bible
Commentary, Revised.* Grand Rapids, Mich.: Wm. B. Eerdmans Publishing Company; London: Inter-Varsity Fellowship,
1970. 1,320 pp.

1st ed., 1953.

In the 1970 edition five of the twelve introductory articles
and thirty-seven of the sixty-six commentaries are entirely new.

Other materials have been extensively revised. The new edition is based on the Revised Standard Version whereas the earlier edition was based on the King James Version. "The general aim of the commentary has remained the same—to provide for the serious student of the Bible a new and up-to-date treatment of the text which combines unqualified belief in its divine inspiration, essential historical trustworthiness and positive Christian usefulness with careful scholarship" (Preface).

216. *The Interpreter's One-Volume Commentary on the Bible;* introduction and commentary for each book of the Bible, including the Apocrypha; with general articles. Charles M. Laymon, ed. Nashville and New York: Abingdon Press, 1971. 1,386 pp.

Independent of *The Interpreter's Bible* (no. 194), this commentary represents the work of Protestant scholars of many denominations plus a few Catholic and Jewish scholars. Intended for ministers, laypersons, and college students, it has numerous illustrations, maps, charts, and an extensive subject index. The general articles, with bibliographies appended, present historical, literary, linguistic, geographical, archaeological, and theological approaches to Biblical interpretation.

217. Blair, Edward P. *Abingdon Bible Handbook.* Nashville and New York: Abingdon Press, 1975. 511 pp.

A popularly written, illustrated, and indexed one-volume handbook presenting brief introductory articles on the Bible as a whole as well as on individual books of the Bible. Most handbooks, often called "introductions," usually deal with only the Old Testament or the New Testament, and often from a more technical and scholarly point of view. This work is useful to the layperson and Bible teacher in the parish.

ATLASES

Listed here in chronological order by date of publication are some of the more recent atlases of the Bible lands.

218. Grollenberg, Lucas Hendricus. *Atlas of the Bible.* Tr. and ed. by Joyce M. H. Reid and H. H. Rowley. London and New York: Thomas Nelson & Sons, 1956. 165 pp. (Oversize.)

The work of a Catholic scholar, first published in Dutch in

1954 and then in French. A historical atlas containing easily read maps, over 400 attractive black-and-white photographs, and text that unites the two. Includes an index of places and persons. Presents a wealth of reliable information; useful to both the general reader and the specialist.

219. Kraeling, Emil G. *Rand McNally Bible Atlas.* New York: Rand McNally & Company, 1956. 487 pp.

Contains twenty-two colored maps in the center of the volume. Text with some black-and-white photographs as well as line maps makes up the rest of the book. The text follows the order of the Old Testament historical books, Genesis through Nehemiah; the order of the Gospel of Mark and the book of Acts in the New Testament. Place name index and subject index are appended. Intended for the general reader.

220. Wright, George E., and Filson, Floyd V. *The Westminster Historical Atlas to the Bible.* Rev. ed. Philadelphia: The Westminster Press, 1956. 130 pp. (Oversize.)

1st ed., 1945.

Text, maps, and illustrations have been revised. Attractive colored maps with text accompanying each one. The scholarly text is among the best of the recent historical atlases. Includes indexes to the text, to the maps, and to Arabic names.

221. Aharoni, Yohanan, and Avi-Yonah, Michael. *The Macmillan Bible Atlas.* New York: The Macmillan Company; London: Collier-Macmillan, 1968. 184 pp.

Prepared by two professors of archaeology at the Hebrew University of Jerusalem, this work contains 264 maps of Biblical events accompanied by descriptive text "to show the changes and historical processes in the lands of the Bible" (Preface). It concentrates on the Holy Land and does not attempt to be an atlas of the Ancient East or of the Hellenistic and Roman Empires. Includes illustrations and index.

222. Negenman, Jan H. *New Atlas of the Bible.* Edited by Harold H. Rowley and translated by Hubert Hoskins and Richard Beckley. Garden City, N.J.: Doubleday & Company, Inc., 1969. 208 pp. (Oversize.)

Originally published in Dutch in 1968, this attractive work "traces in broad outline the growth of the Bible in the setting of the history out of which each of its parts came" (Foreword).

Magnificent photographs and maps in both black and white and color. Epilogue, pp. 194–200, by Lucas H. Grollenberg.

223. *Atlas of Israel;* cartography, physical geography, human and economic geography, history. Jerusalem: Survey of Israel, Minister of Labor; Amsterdam: Elsevier Publishing Co., 1970. No paging.

Originally published in Hebrew, 1956–1964. A massive, authoritative work dealing both with contemporary Israel and its historical origins. Sections include, among others: geology, climate, hydrology, botany, zoology, land utilization, history. Numerous colored maps, charts, statistics. Useful to the student of the Bible.

224. Baly, Denis, and Tushingham, A.D. *Atlas of the Biblical World.* New York: World Publishing Company, 1971. 208 pp.

Differs from many other Bible atlases as its primary emphasis is on geography rather than history. Includes also two chapters with archaeological orientation. Scope is the entire Middle East rather than only Palestine. Numerous maps and photographs in color and black and white. Bibliography, text index, and map index provided.

225. May, Herbert G., ed. *Oxford Bible Atlas.* 2d ed. London and New York: Oxford University Press, 1974. 144 pp.

1st ed., 1962.

A small, though extremely useful, historical atlas with colored maps and accompanying text; also numerous black-and-white photographs. A chapter on "Archaeology and the Bible" by R. W. Hamilton and a gazetteer are appended.

CHAPTER IV

Parts of the Bible

THE OLD TESTAMENT

BIBLIOGRAPHY

226. Childs, Brevard S. *Old Testament Books for Pastor and Teacher.* Philadelphia: The Westminster Press, 1977. 120 pp.

A bibliographic essay by a leading American Old Testament scholar. Provides critical notes and recommendations for purchase of Old Testament exegetical tools. Gives primary emphasis to the evaluation of commentaries of individual books of the Old Testament. Also includes a bibliography, arranged alphabetically by author, of all works included in the essay, and an appendix listing secondhand bookstores.

227. Society for Old Testament Study. *Book List.* Manchester, 1945 to date. Annual.

Contains short reviews by British scholars of the year's important books in Old Testament from throughout the world. These annual lists up until 1973 have been bound together, although not cumulated, in the following three volumes:

Rowley, H. H., ed. *Eleven Years of Bible Bibliography.* London: Falcon's Wing, 1957. 804 pp.

Anderson, G. W., ed. *A Decade of Bible Bibliography.* Oxford: Basil Blackwell & Mott, Ltd., 1967. 706 pp.

Ackroyd, Peter R. *Bible Bibliography, 1967–1973; Old Testament.* Oxford: Basil Blackwell & Mott, Ltd., 1974. 505 pp.

228. Buss, Martin J. *Old Testament Dissertations, 1928–1958.* 57 pp.

Privately printed. Contains bibliographic information on North American dissertations before *Dissertation Abstracts International* (no. 90) began coverage. Also contains sections on

dissertations written in the British Isles, pp. 31–33, and elsewhere, pp. 34–57.

TEXT

229. Kittel, Rudolf, ed. *Biblia Hebraica.* 14th ed. Stuttgart:
Württembergische Bibelanstalt, 1966.
The standard critical edition of the Old Testament text.

GRAMMARS

230. Gesenius, Heinrich Friedrich Wilhelm. *Gesenius' Hebrew Grammar.* Edited and enlarged by E. Kautzsch. 2d English ed., revised by A. E. Crowley. Oxford: Clarendon Press,
1910. 598 pp.
The standard advanced Hebrew grammar; often reprinted.
231. Lambdin, Thomas O. *Introduction to Biblical Hebrew.*
New York: Charles Scribner's Sons, 1971. 345 pp.
Less detailed than Gesenius, but probably too detailed for the
beginner.

LEXICONS

232. Brown, Francis; Driver, S. R.; and Briggs, Charles A.
A Hebrew and English Lexicon of the Old Testament; with an
appendix containing the Biblical Aramaic, based on the lexicon
of William Gesenius as translated by Edward Robinson. Oxford: Clarendon Press, 1957. 1,127 pp.
1st ed., 1907. Reprinted with corrections, 1953, 1957.
Old, but still useful and basic for the English-speaking student.
233. Einspahr, Bruce. *Index to the Brown, Driver and Briggs
Hebrew Lexicon.* Chicago: Moody Press, 1976. 452 pp.
Lists each Hebrew word by book, chapter, and verse; gives
English translation, with page and section where the word may
be found in Brown, Driver, and Briggs. Computer-produced. Of
help to the student whose command of Hebrew is less than
certain.
234. Koehler, Ludwig, and Baumgartner, Walter. *Lexicon in*

Veteris Testamenti Libros. 2d ed. Leiden: E. J. Brill, 1958.

More up-to-date technically than Brown, Driver, and Briggs (no. 232), but the English translation from the German edition is not always of the highest quality.

CONCORDANCES

235. Mandelkern, Solomon. *Veteris Testamenti Concordantiae Hebraicae atque Chaldaicae.* Graz, Austria: Akademische Druck und Verlagsanstalt, 1955. 2 vols.

Originally published 1896.

The Graz reprint is of the 1937 edition published by Schocken. The most comprehensive Hebrew concordance.

236. Wigram, George V. *The Englishman's Hebrew and Chaldee Concordance of the Old Testament;* being an attempt at a verbal connection between the original and the English translation. 3d ed. London: Bagster, 1874. 2 vols. (Reprint: Grand Rapids, Mich.: Zondervan Publishing House, 1970.)

Under the Hebrew word, lists in English translation the passages where that word is used. Useful to the student with little command of Hebrew.

SEPTUAGINT

237. Brock, Sebastian P.; Fritsch, Charles T.; and Jellicoe, Sidney. *A Classified Bibliography of the Septuagint.* Leiden: E. J. Brill, 1973. 217 pp. (Arbeiten zur Literatur und Geschichte des hellenistischen Judentums, VI.)

"Coverage is down to 1969 (inclusive), but at the other end of the scale it has seemed preferable not to impose any rigid starting point, hence the practice has been to be increasingly selective for the literature prior to 1900, and it is only in exceptional cases that items earlier than c. 1860 are included" (Introduction).

238. Rahlfs, Alfred. *Septuaginta, id est, Vetus Testamentum Graece Iuxta LXX Interpretes.* 8th ed. Stuttgart: Württembergische Bibelanstalt, 1965. 2 vols.

A critical edition containing also a brief summary in German, English, and Latin of the history of the Septuagint.

239. *The Septuagint Version of the Old Testament with an English Translation.* London: Bagster, 1896. 1,130 and 248 pp. (Reprint: Grand Rapids, Mich.: Zondervan Publishing House, 1972.)

Not a critical text, but convenient to use. Includes the Apocrypha.

240. Hatch, Edwin, and Redpath, Henry A. *A Concordance to the Septuagint and the Other Greek Versions of the Old Testament (Including the Apocryphal Books).* Graz, Austria: Akademische Druck und Verlagsanstalt, 1954. 2 vols. and Supplement.

Reprinted from the Clarendon Press edition of 1897–1906.

INTRODUCTIONS

241. *Guides to Biblical Scholarship.* Gene M. Tucker, ed. Philadelphia: Fortress Press, 1971 ff. (In progress.)

A continuing series of brief but critical treatments by leading authorities on such issues as form criticism, tradition criticism, and literary criticism. For appraisal of the standard critical and conservative introductions, see Childs (no. 226), pp. 22–23.

COMMENTARY SERIES

Listed here are three commentary series dealing only with the Old Testament. Other series with works on both the Old Testament and the New Testament are listed in nos. 193–217. For a detailed evaluation of both series of commentaries and individual commentaries on Old Testament books by a specialist, see Childs (no. 226), pp. 31–88.

242. *The Old Testament Library.* G. Ernest Wright, John Bright, James Barr, Peter Ackroyd, gen. eds. Philadelphia: The Westminster Press; London: SCM Press, Ltd. 1961 ff.

Scholarly works by leading American, British, and Continental authorities. As these works are intended for the nontheologian as well as for the specialist, limits are set on the discussion of philological and archaeological problems.

243. *The New International Commentary on the Old Testament.* R. K. Harrison, gen. ed. Grand Rapids, Mich.: Wm. B.

Eerdmans Publishing Company, 1965 ff.

A scholarly series written from a conservative orientation. Each volume includes introduction, translation, exposition, notes, and extensive bibliography.

244. *The Tyndale Old Testament Commentaries.* D. J. Wiseman, gen. ed. London: Inter-Varsity Fellowship, 1974 ff.

Intended to "provide the student of the Bible with a handy, up-to-date commentary on each book, with the primary emphasis on exegesis. Major critical questions are discussed in the introductions and additional notes, while undue technicalities have been avoided" (General Preface in *Deuteronomy*). No text printed. Authors quote from various versions or give their own translations. Conservative in perspective, but more popularly written than *The New International Commentary on the Old Testament* (no. 243).

THE NEW TESTAMENT

BIBLIOGRAPHY OF THE WHOLE NEW TESTAMENT

The study of the New Testament receives good bibliographic coverage in the tools concerned with the whole Bible listed in nos. 127–139. However, there are also several specifically New Testament bibliographic tools, both retrospective and current, which are most useful.

245. Hurd, John Coolidge, Jr. *A Bibliography of New Testament Bibliographies.* New York: The Seabury Press, Inc., 1966. 75 pp.

A classified list of bibliographies, both those separately published as well as those appearing as parts of books or in journal articles. Some annotations as well as indication of time period covered by the bibliographies listed. Includes a chapter on biographies and bibliographies of New Testament scholars.

246. San Francisco Theological Seminary. *Bibliography of New Testament Literature, 1900–1950.* San Anselmo, Calif.: San Francisco Theological Seminary, 1954. 312 pp.

Prepared by a graduate seminar under the direction of John Wick Bowman and edited by Tadasha Akaishi. A classified arrangement, with annotations and index, of some 2,400 books and some periodical articles in English. The journals indexed cover 1920–1950 and include only the *Expository Times, Harvard Theological Review, Interpretation, Journal of Biblical Literature, Journal of Religion,* and *Journal of Theological Studies.*

247. Lyons, William Nelson, ed. *New Testament Literature in 1940.* Chicago: New Testament Club of the University of Chicago, 1941. 34 pp.

Classified arrangement, evaluative as well as descriptive annotations; no index, few European materials cited.

————. *New Testament Literature in 1941.* 78 pp.

Parvis, Merrill M., ed. *New Testament Literature in 1942.* 107 pp.

248. Lyons, William Nelson, and Parvis, Merrill M. *New Testament Literature; An Annotated Bibliography* (1943–1945). Chicago: The University of Chicago Press, 1948. 392 pp.

Classified, annotated, indexed. While this work and its earlier editions (no. 247) cover only 1940–1945, additional New Testament bibliography before and after this period may be found in *Elenchus Bibliographicus Biblicus* (no. 138), published in *Biblica* beginning in 1920. From 1949 the *Index to Religious Periodical Literature* (no. 43) also includes New Testament bibliography.

249. Metzger, Bruce M. *Index of Articles on the New Testament and the Early Church Published in Festschriften.* Philadelphia: Society of Biblical Literature, 1951. 182 pp. (Journal of Biblical Literature Monograph Series, V.)

————. ————. *Supplement,* 1955. 20 pp.

The main volume and the Supplement index 640 Festschriften, i.e., memorial or homage works presented to a scholar or an institution. Arranged in classified order with author index; includes works published through 1950.

250. *New Testament Abstracts:* a record of current periodical literature. 1956 to date. Cambridge, Mass.: Weston College School of Theology, in cooperation with the Council on the Study of Religion, 1956 to date. 3 times a year.

Includes résumés in English of journal articles and books in various languages. In classified order with annual index of principal Scripture texts, index of authors, index of book reviews, and index of book notices. A cumulative index to Vols. 1–15

(1956–1971) was published in 1974. Currently indexes over 380 scholarly journals. While under Catholic sponsorship, it is ecumenical as well as international in its coverage. A basic tool for current literature in New Testament studies.

251. Scholer, David M. *A Basic Bibliographic Guide for New Testament Exegesis.* 2d ed. Grand Rapids, Mich.: Wm. B. Eerdmans Publishing Company, 1973. 94 pp.

A brief guide, with some annotations, to basic tools; in classified order with author index.

BIBLIOGRAPHY OF PARTS OF THE NEW TESTAMENT

252. Metzger, Bruce M. *Index to Periodical Literature on Christ and the Gospels.* Leiden: E. J. Brill, 1966. 602 pp. (New Testament Tools and Studies, VI.)

Indexes in classified order 10,090 articles from the complete runs of 160 periodicals written in sixteen languages through 1961. Includes index of authors.

253. Malatesta, Edward. *St. John's Gospel, 1920–1965:* a cumulative and classified bibliography of books and periodical literature on the Fourth Gospel. Rome: Pontifical Biblical Institute, 1967. 205 pp. (Analecta Biblica, No. 32.)

A compilation from some fifty volumes of *Elenchus Bibliographicus Biblicus* (no. 138) of materials related to the Gospel of John; includes books, articles, and book reviews.

254. Kissinger, Warren S. *The Sermon on the Mount:* a history of interpretation and bibliography. Metuchen, N.J.: Scarecrow Press, Inc., and American Theological Library Association, 1975. 296 pp.

Includes an extensive essay on the history of the interpretation of the Sermon on the Mount (pp. 1–125) and a bibliography of Sermon on the Mount texts, criticism, interpretations, sermons, meditations, etc. Separate section for the Beatitudes. Works in many languages and from many confessions included. Biblical reference index and general index provided.

255. Mattill, Andrew Jacob, and Mattill, Mary Bedford. *A Classified Bibliography of Literature on the Acts of the Apostles.* Leiden: E. J. Brill, 1966. 513 pp. (New Testament Tools and Studies, VII.)

Includes 6,646 entries in many languages of books and articles appearing in over 180 periodicals through 1961. Arranged in classified order with an index of authors. The longest chapter (pp. 322–475) is on exegetical studies of individual passages. Excluded are New Testament introductions and theologies, book reviews, homiletical and devotional works, and articles in dictionaries and encyclopedias.

256. Pittsburgh Theological Seminary. *A Periodical and Monographic Index to the Literature of the Gospels and Acts.* Pittsburgh: The Clifford E. Barbour Library, 1971. 330 pp. (Bibliographia Tripotamopolitana, III.)

A reproduction of the shelf list of the École Biblique in Jerusalem (see no. 136). Arrangement of entries follows the order of the chapters and verses of the four Gospels and Acts. Covers a period of eighty years of Biblical scholarship through 1968. Supplements Mattill (no. 255), which includes entries only up until 1961. One fourth of the École Biblique entries on Acts are from the 1962–1968 period.

257. Metzger, Bruce M. *Index to Periodical Literature on the Apostle Paul.* Grand Rapids, Mich.: Wm. B. Eerdmans Publishing Company, 1951. 183 pp. (New Testament Tools and Studies, I.)

Lists 2,987 articles on the apostle Paul appearing anywhere in the complete runs of over one hundred periodicals in fourteen languages. Classified arrangement with an author index.

BIBLIOGRAPHY OF SPECIAL SUBJECTS
RELATED TO THE NEW TESTAMENT

258. Metzger, Bruce M. *Annotated Bibliography of the Textual Criticism of the New Testament, 1914–1939.* Copenhagen: Einar Munksgaard Forlag, 1955. 133 pp. (Studies and Documents, XVIII.)

Lists in classified order, and sometimes annotates, 1,188 books, monographs, studies, dissertations, and articles culled from searching 236 periodicals and serials in many languages. Index of names provided. *Theologischer Jahresbericht* surveyed literature on textual criticism regularly until 1914 and the New Testament Club of the University of Chicago published bibliographies covering this field from 1940 through 1945 (nos. 247, 248). For later coverage, see *Elenchus Bibliographicus Biblicus* (no. 138) and the *Index to Religious Periodical Literature* (no. 43).

259. Doty, William G. *The Discipline and Literature of New Testament Form Criticism;* a bibliographical lecture. Evanston, Ill.: Garrett Theological Seminary Library, 1967. 24 pp.

Lists in classified order 215 major and minor articles and books that supply an overview of early form critics, subsequent developments, criticisms, and new directions. No index.

260. Nickels, Peter. *Targum and New Testament:* a bibliography together with a New Testament index. Rome: Pontifical Biblical Institute, 1967. 88 pp.

A listing of works in which New Testament texts are treated in relation to Aramaic versions of the Old Testament. Part I lists separately published books and articles in alphabetical order; Part II lists most of the items in Part I in the order of the chapters and verses of the New Testament writings to which they relate.

TEXTS

261. Nestle, Eberhard; Nestle, Erwin; and Aland, Kurt, eds. *Novum Testamentum Graece.* 25th ed. Stuttgart: Württembergische Bibelanstalt, 1963. 571 pp.

1st ed. edited by Eberhard Nestle in 1898. Later editions edited by Nestle's son, Erwin, and by Kurt Aland, who will succeed the latter as editor.

The text is eclectic, based on the critical editions of Tischendorf and Westcott and Hort, as well as on manuscript evidence. An elaborate critical apparatus is immensely useful to the exegete. Danker (no. 127), pp. 19–42, has a most helpful chapter on the use of the critical apparatus. The Nestle-Aland work is the basic critical text in handy pocket size for serious exegetical study.

262. Aland, Kurt; Black, Matthew; Martini, Carlo M.; Metzger, Bruce M.; and Wikgren, Allen, eds. *The Greek New Testament.* 3d ed. New York, London, Edinburgh, Amsterdam, Stuttgart: United Bible Societies, 1975. 918 pp.

Intended for the use of Bible translators, this text was the work of several Bible societies in the United States, England, Scotland, the Netherlands, and Germany. It is not intended to replace the more detailed Nestle-Aland edition. The *Good News Bible: The Bible in Today's English Version* (no. 179) used this text for its New Testament translation.

GRAMMARS

263. Machen, J. Gresham. *New Testament Greek for Beginners.* New York: The Macmillan Company, 1923. 287 pp.
Often reprinted and still widely used.

264. Blass, F., and Debrunner, A. *A Greek Grammar of the New Testament and Other Early Christian Literature.* A translation and revision of the ninth-tenth German edition . . . by Robert W. Funk. Chicago: The University of Chicago Press, 1961. 325 pp.
A more advanced reference work. Includes index of subjects, index of Greek words and forms of the New Testament and other early Christian literature.

LEXICONS

265. Bauer, Walter. *A Greek-English Lexicon of the New Testament and Other Early Christian Literature.* Translated and adapted from 4th rev. and augmented edition, 1952, by William F. Arndt and F. Wilbur Gingrich. Chicago: The University of Chicago, Press, 1957. 909 pp.
Popularly cited as "Bauer-Arndt-Gingrich," this is the standard complete New Testament lexicon in English.

266. Souter, Alexander. *A Pocket Lexicon to the Greek New Testament.* Oxford: Clarendon Press, 1916. 290 pp.
A brief, handy tool for ready reference.

CONCORDANCES

267. Moulton, W. F., and Geden, A. S., eds. *A Concordance to the Greek Testament,* according to the texts of Westcott and Hort, Tischendorf, and the English revisers. 4th ed., revised by

H. K. Moulton. New York: Charles Scribner's Sons, 1963. 1,033 pp.

1st ed., 1897.

The standard complete New Testament Greek concordance.

268. Schmoller, Alfred. *Handkonkordanz zum griechischen Neuen Testament.* 14th ed. Stuttgart: Württembergische Bibelanstalt, 1968.

Smaller than Moulton-Geden (no. 267); incomplete, but useful.

269. Morrison, Clinton. *An Analytical Concordance to the Revised Standard Version of the New Testament.* Philadelphia: The Westminster Press, 1979. xxv and 773 pp.

A work of outstanding erudition that will serve the readers of the New Testament of the RSV as Young's (no. 182) and Strong's (no. 183) concordances served the readers of the King James Version. It is intended for the English reader, but will prove equally valuable for the Greek reader. It differs from *Nelson's Complete Concordance of the Revised Standard Version Bible* (no. 185) in that it is "analytical," i.e., it lists under each English word used in the RSV the various Greek words translated by that one English word. It is also "exhaustive" as it omits only the four most common New Testament Greek words, those normally translated by "the," "and," "but," and "self, he, she, it." It includes an index-lexicon based on the Greek New Testament with transliteration, thus making it fully accessible to the English reader, and also a wealth of notes and appendixes on the analysis of the RSV and its revisions.

VERSIONS AND TRANSLATIONS

270. Weymouth, Richard Francis. *The New Testament in Modern Speech.* London: J. Clarke, 1903.

Revised by James A. Robertson, 1927. Based on the translator's own edition of the Greek text, this work is noted for its carefulness in rendering the shades of meaning of the Greek tenses. Includes footnotes and section headings. Weymouth intended this translation to "furnish a succinct and compressed running commentary (not doctrinal) to be used side by side with its elder compeers" (Preface). He also hoped it would stimulate interest in producing a satisfactory English Bible to supersede the Authorized Version and the Revised Version.

271. Montgomery, Helen Barrett. *The New Testament in Modern English.* Valley Forge, Pa.: Judson Press, 1924.

The only New Testament translation done entirely by a woman, this work aims "to offer a translation in the language of everyday life, that does not depart too much from the translations already familiar and beloved" (Introduction).

272. *The Authentic New Testament;* Edited and translated from the Greek for the general reader by Hugh J. Schonfield. London: Dobson Books, Ltd., 1955.

A translation of the New Testament done by a Jew. Attempts to use nontraditional, nonecclesiastical language in conveying the meaning of the New Testament in its original Jewish and Hellenistic context. Verse and chapter divisions have been dropped.

273. Williams, Charles Kingsley. *The New Testament; A New Translation in Plain English.* Grand Rapids, Mich.: Wm. B. Eerdmans Publishing Company, 1963.

Translated from the Greek text underlying the Revised Version New Testament (1881) by a British educator and missionary, this work is intended for those for whom English is a second language. The text is printed in paragraph form, except for poetic passages, which are in verse form. Long sentences in the Greek are broken up into shorter English sentences. Notes and glossary are appended.

274. Phillips, J. B. *The New Testament in Modern English.* New York: The Macmillan Company, 1958.

A highly popular translation that began in 1947 with *Letters to Young Churches* and was completed in 1958. In 1963 *Four Prophets: Amos, Hosea, First Isaiah, Micah* appeared. Phillips sets three tests for a good translation: it must not sound like a translation; it must reveal the least possible obtrusion of the translator's personality; it should be able to produce in the readers an effect equivalent to that produced by the author upon his original readers. Phillips, a British scholar, does well in all three tests. His is not a word-for-word translation, but rather a conveying-of-meaning translation, sometimes considered even a paraphrase. While not intended for liturgical use, it is most valuable for personal reading and study.

275. Barclay, William. *The New Testament, A New Translation.* London and New York: William Collins Sons & Co., Ltd., 1968–1969. 2 vols.

Vol. 1, The Gospels and the Acts of the Apostles; Vol. 2, The Letters and the Revelation.

Barclay, one of the most popular Biblical commentators writing especially for the layperson, states that his aim was "to try to make the New Testament intelligible to the man who is not a technical scholar" and "to try to make a translation which did not need a commentary to explain it" (Foreword). Prose is printed in paragraph form and poetry in verse form. Vol. 1 contains an essay "On Translating the New Testament," pp. 308–352. Vol. 2 contains definitions and discussion of "New Testament Words," pp. 340–350, in which Barclay discusses the passages where he felt it was necessary to paraphrase to convey the meaning accurately. A most useful translation for both personal and group Bible study.

276. *The Translator's New Testament.* London: British and Foreign Bible Society, 1973.

Intended for those who translate the New Testament into the language of their mother tongue and depend upon English for the materials of Biblical scholarship. It serves as a bridge between the United Bible Societies' Greek text (no. 262) and the language into which the New Testament is being translated. This is the work of a team of thirty-five British New Testament scholars and missionary linguists. Translational notes and glossary are appended. Useful not only for translators but also for students or clergy who desire a clear, concise translation, arranged in paragraph form.

277. Marshall, Alfred. *The Revised Standard Version Interlinear Greek-English New Testament;* The Nestle Greek text with a literal English translation. London: Samuel Bagster & Sons, Ltd., 1968. Grand Rapids, Mich.: Zondervan Publishing House, 1970.

Includes a foreword by J. B. Phillips and marginal text of the RSV. The same interlinear translation with a marginal text of the King James Version was published by Bagster in 1958 and reprinted by Zondervan in 1975. In 1975 Zondervan also printed the same interlinear translation with both the King James Version and the *New International Version.*

278. Weigle, Luther A., ed. *The New Testament Octapla;* Eight English versions of the New Testament in the Tyndale-King James tradition. New York: Thomas Nelson & Sons, 1962.

Contains in parallel columns the texts of the following versions (given in parentheses are date of original publication and date of revision or edition represented): *Tyndale* (1525/1535), *Great Bible* (1539/1540), *Geneva Bible* (1560/1562), *Bishop's Bible* (1568/1602), *Rheims* (1582), King James (1611/1873), American Standard (1881/1901), and Revised Standard (1946/1960) versions.

COMMENTARY SERIES

279. *Cambridge Greek Testament for Schools and Colleges.* Cambridge: University Press, 1881–1914. 19 vols.

Includes introductions, maps, and brief, succinct notes on words and phrases of the Greek New Testament. Emphasizes questions of authenticity, history, and philology.

280. *Cambridge Greek Testament Commentary.* C. F. D. Moule, gen. ed. Cambridge: University Press, 1955 ff.

Continues the high scholarly standards of the earlier series, but gives more attention to the theological and religious contents of the New Testament than to historical and linguistic questions.

281. *The Expositor's Greek Testament.* W. Robertson Nicoll, ed. New York: Dodd, Mead, 1897–1910. 5 vols. (Reprint: Grand Rapids, Mich.: Wm. B. Eerdmans Publishing Company, 1974.)

Intended to replace Henry Alford's *The Greek Testament* (London, 1849–1860, 4 vols.). Detailed exegesis of the Greek text; should be supplemented with more recent works.

282. *The Moffatt New Testament Commentary.* James Moffatt, ed. London: Hodder & Stoughton, Ltd.; New York: Harper & Brothers, 1926–1950. 17 vols.

Based on Moffatt's *A New Translation of the Bible* (no. 172). Aims "to bring out the religious meaning and message of the New Testament writings" (Editor's Preface). Does not require knowledge of the Greek. Provides running commentary on the text rather than verse-by-verse notes. Has proven to be an extremely popular series. Includes such contributors as E. F. Scott (Ephesians), F. J. Foakes-Jackson (Acts), C. H. Dodd (Johannine epistles).

283. *The New International Commentary on the New Testament.* F. F. Bruce, gen. ed. Grand Rapids, Mich.: Wm. B. Eerdmans Publishing Company, 1951 ff.

Ned B. Stonehouse was general editor until his death in 1962, when F. F. Bruce succeeded him. Represents scholarly conservative, Reformed point of view.

284. Barclay, William. *The Daily Study Bible.* Rev. ed. Philadelphia: The Westminster Press, 1975–1976.

1st ed., 1952–1960.

Written at the request of the Church of Scotland for use among its members, this series has won popularity throughout the English-speaking world. Includes translation, introduction, and interpretation. An index volume was published in 1978.

285. *Black's New Testament Commentaries.* Henry Chadwick, gen. ed. London: A. & C. Black, Ltd., 1957 ff.

In the United States, several volumes of this series are published by Harper & Row under the title *Harper's New Testament Commentaries.*

Falling between the technical and the popular commentaries, this series draws upon prominent New Testament scholars on both sides of the Atlantic as its contributors. Includes introductions, translation, and commentary. Knowledge of Greek is not required for its use.

286. *The Tyndale New Testament Commentaries.* R. V. G. Tasker, gen. ed. Grand Rapids, Mich.: Wm. B. Eerdmans Publishing Company, 1957–1974. 20 vols.

Popularly written series based on the King James Version; produced by "a number of scholars who, while they are free to make their own individual contributions, are united in a common desire to promote a truly biblical theology" (General Preface).

THEOLOGICAL DICTIONARY

287. Kittel, Gerhard, ed. *Theological Dictionary of the New Testament.* Translated and edited by Geoffrey W. Bromiley. Grand Rapids, Mich.: Wm. B. Eerdmans Publishing Company, 1964–1976. 10 vols.

Translated from the German; Vols. 1–5 edited by Gerhard Kittel; Vols. 6–9 edited by Gerhard Friedrich; Vol. 10, Index volume, compiled by Ronald E. Pitkin.

A standard work with long articles, some of monograph length, that discuss theologically significant New Testament terms. Articles include relevant usage in the Old Testament, in Judaism, and in Hellenistic literature. The recently published index volume facilitates the use of the whole work, especially for those with limited knowledge of Greek or Hebrew. Includes indexes of English key words, Greek key words, Hebrew and Aramaic words, and Biblical references as well as biographical information on contributors and an essay on the "Pre-history of the Theological Dictionary of the New Testament."

CHAPTER V

Systematic Theology

Systematic theology does not have the mass of bibliographic and reference tools that are available for Biblical studies. However, in addition to the works listed in this chapter, the general theological encyclopedias and dictionaries (nos. 96–101) also provide articles and bibliography in systematic theology.

COMPREHENSIVE PROTESTANT HANDBOOKS AND DICTIONARIES

288. *A Handbook of Christian Theology:* definition essays on concepts and movements of thought in contemporary Protestantism. Cleveland and New York: The World Publishing Company, 1958. 380 pp.

Consists of 101 brief signed essays written by leading American and European Protestant scholars; arranged in alphabetical order by title. Reflects Protestant thought in the middle of the twentieth century. Most essays have appended a very brief bibliography.

289. *Baker's Dictionary of Theology.* Everett F. Harrison, ed. in chief; Geoffrey W. Bromiley, assoc. ed.; Carl F. H. Henry, consulting ed. Grand Rapids, Mich.: Baker Book House, 1960. 566 pp.

Brief signed articles with bibliography by conservative American and British scholars. "The articles are formed with a view to acquainting the reader with the tension points in theological discussion today in addition to providing a positive exposition of the biblical content in each case" (Preface).

290. Harvey, Van A. *A Handbook of Theological Terms.* New York: The Macmillan Company, 1964. 253 pp.

The terms discussed are limited to those used in systematic

and philosophical theology. Intended for the serious layperson. Useful also to the student for quick reference.

291. *Christian Word Book.* J. Sherrill Hendricks, Gene E. Sease, Eric Lane Titus, James Bryan Wiggins. Nashville and New York: Abingdon Press, 1968. 320 pp.

Intended for sophisticated youth as well as adults; includes terms used in theology, ethics, Biblical studies, ecclesiology, and worship. Each article is signed by one of the four authors.

292. Richardson, Alan, ed. *A Dictionary of Christian Theology.* Philadelphia: The Westminster Press, 1969. 364 pp.

Brief signed articles, with bibliography, mostly by British scholars; concerned with development of thought rather than with biographical detail or events in church history; concentrates on "interlocking areas of theology and philosophy" (Preface). Intended for the student, minister, layperson, or philosopher who needs information in the area of theology.

COMPREHENSIVE CATHOLIC DICTIONARIES AND ENCYCLOPEDIAS

293. *A Catholic Dictionary of Theology;* a work projected with the approval of the Catholic Hierarchy of England and Wales. London: Thomas Nelson & Sons, Ltd., 1962 ff.

Editorial board includes H. Francis Davis, Aidan Williams, Ivo Thomas, and Joseph Crehan. Intended as a companion to *A Catholic Commentary on Holy Scripture* (no. 210). Three of the four projected volumes have appeared thus far. Contains long, signed, scholarly articles with bibliography; reflects the current renewal of theology in the Catholic Church.

294. Bouyer, Louis. *Dictionary of Theology.* Tr. by Charles Underhill Quinn. Tournai, Belgium: Desclee, 1965. 471 pp.

First published in French in 1963. Provides brief, concise definitions of theological terms for laypersons, students, preachers, and catechists. Frequent reference is made to Biblical texts and texts of the Catholic Church magisterium, and to Thomas Aquinas. Limited to dogmatic theology. An appendix lists articles topically to conform to the sequence of doctrines presented in the Apostles' Creed. More traditional in approach than Rahner's work (no. 295).

295. Rahner, Karl, and Vorgrimler, Herbert. *Theological*

Dictionary. Ed. by Cornelius Ernst and tr. by Richard Strachan. New York: Herder & Herder, Inc., 1965. 493 pp.

First published in German in 1961. Short articles explaining the concepts of Catholic dogmatic theology in contemporary and often existential vocabulary. Readers must be prepared "to make a certain intellectual effort" (Author's Preface). Serves as a useful complement to Bouyer's work (no. 294).

296. *Sacramentum Mundi;* an encyclopedia of theology. Ed. by Karl Rahner (and others). New York: Herder & Herder, Inc., 1968–1970. 6 vols.

A post-Vatican II work, published simultaneously in English, Dutch, French, German, Italian, and Spanish; contributors include Catholic scholars from many countries. Consists of long, signed articles, with bibliography, that present current Catholic thought in theology. Is marked by "its openness for the other Christian Churches, the non-Christian religions and for the world in general" (General Preface). A general index is included in Vol. 6.

297. *Encyclopedia of Theology: The Concise Sacramentum Mundi.* Karl Rahner, ed. New York: The Seabury Press, Inc., 1975. 1,841 pp.

Contains revisions of the major articles on theology, Biblical studies, and related topics from *Sacramentum Mundi* (no. 296), *Lexikon für Theologie und Kirche,* and *Theologisches Taschenlexikon.* Bibliographies are omitted. Intended for the student and the general public as a basic encyclopedia of Christian theology for the modern age. Most useful for ready reference.

THOMISTIC STUDIES

298. *Rassegna di Letteratura Tomistica. Thomistic Bulletin. Boletín Tomista. Thomistische Literaturschau.* 1966 to date. Naples: Edizioni Dominicane Italiane, 1969 to date. Annual.

A classified, annotated bibliography listing works in the common international languages on the person, writings, doctrine, and influence of Thomas Aquinas. Date of publication is about three years after the date of the works listed.

CHRISTOLOGY

299. Ayres, Samuel Gardiner. *Jesus Christ Our Lord;* an English bibliography of Christology comprising over five thousand titles annotated and classified. New York: Armstrong, 1906. 502 pp.

Classified order with subject index and author index. Annotations consist of brief notes at the beginning of each section. Includes devotional as well as scholarly works.

300. Case, Adelaide Teague. *As Modern Writers See Jesus;* a descriptive bibliography of books about Jesus. Boston and Chicago: Pilgrim Press, 1927. 119 pp.

Provides longer annotations of both popular and scholarly works, most of them written within the decade preceding publication of this bibliography. Index of titles and index of authors appended.

ECCLESIOLOGY

301. *Répertoire Bibliographique des Institutions Chrétiennes. Bibliographical Repertory of Christian Institutions.* Vols. 2 ff., 1968 to date. René Metz and Jean Schlick, eds. Strasbourg: Centre de Recherche et de Documentation des Institutions Chrétiennes (CERDIC), 1969 to date.

Now titled simply *RIC.* An annual computer-produced index of current books and articles in five languages from countries, confessions, and churches throughout the world. As the title indicates, the materials indexed concern the life and work of the church rather than its theology proper. Arranged by country, alphabetically within countries. Use of the general index is essential. A nine-character combination number and letter coding system indicates for each entry its relative importance, whether it contains a bibliography, the confession it deals with, its country of origin, and its identification number.

302. Metz, René, and Schlick, Jean, eds. *RIC Supplement.* Strasbourg: CERDIC, 1973 to date.

A series of subject bibliographies, arranged alphabetically, listing recent books and articles on such themes as marriage and divorce, church and state, armed forces and churches, the Jesus movement, evangelization and mission, liberation and salvation, politics and faith, religious life, etc.

303. Guitard, André, and Litalien, Rolland. *Bibliographie sur le Sacerdoce, 1966–1968.* Montreal: Office National du Clergé, 1969–1970. 6 vols.

Contents: Vol. 1, Bibliographie sur la vocation et la formation sacerdotale; Vol. 2, Bibliographie sur l'épiscopat; Vol. 3, Bibliographie sur le sacerdoce et la vie des prêtres; Vol. 4, Bibliographie sur le ministère sacerdotal et la pastorale; Vol. 5, Bibliographie sur le célibat, l'obéissance et la pauvreté; Vol. 6, Bibliographie sur le diaconat.

Each volume is arranged in classified order with an author index. Many English-language titles are listed. Books and articles included.

304. *Bibliographie Internationale sur le Sacerdoce et le Ministère. International Bibliography on the Priesthood and the Ministry, 1969.* André Guitard and Marie-Georges Bulteau, eds. Montreal: Sacerdoce et Ministère, Centre de Documentation et de Recherche, 1971. 396 pp.

While Catholic in origin, this work is ecumenical and international in coverage of current books and articles. Classified arrangement. Subject headings and index of topics are given in French and English. Also includes an author index.

305. World Council of Churches. Department on the Laity. *Laici in Ecclesia.* Geneva, 1961. 107 pp.

Lists in alphabetical order by author 1,422 books, articles, reports, and pamphlets on the laity in the church. Materials listed are mainly Protestant, published since 1945, and in various languages. Much English-language material listed. Subject index appended.

ESCHATOLOGY

306. Abbot, Ezra. "The Literature of the Doctrine of a Future Life; or, A catalogue of works relating to the nature, origin and destiny of the soul," published in *History of the Doctrine of a Future Life,* 10th ed., by William R. Alger (Boston: Roberts, 1880), pp. 773–1008. Also published separately.

Classified arrangement, chronologically within subject; annotated. Indexes of authors and subjects appended.

ETHICS

307. Ferm, Vergilius, ed. *Encyclopedia of Morals.* New York: Philosophical Library, 1956. 682 pp. (Reprint: New York: Greenwood Press, Inc., 1969.)

Treats both moral theory as propounded by various philosophers and religions as well as moral behavior, especially as it has been studied by anthropologists. Includes cross-references and a name index. Bibliographies appended to articles.

308. Macquarrie, John, ed. *Dictionary of Christian Ethics.* Philadelphia: The Westminster Press, 1967. 366 pp.

Treats basic ethical concepts, Biblical and theological ethics, and substantial ethical problems. Concise signed articles, with bibliography, written by eighty American and British scholars.

309. *Baker's Dictionary of Christian Ethics.* Carl F. H. Henry, ed. Grand Rapids, Mich.: Baker Book House, 1973. 726 pp.

The work of evangelical scholars in the United States and Europe. Signed articles with bibliographies.

CHAPTER VI

Church History

GENERAL CHURCH HISTORY

BIBLIOGRAPHY

310. Case, Shirley Jackson, ed. *A Bibliographical Guide to the History of Christianity.* Compiled by S. J. Case, J. T. McNeill, W. W. Sweet, W. Pauck, M. Spinka. Chicago: The University of Chicago Press, 1931. 265 pp. (Reprint: New York, Peter Smith, 1951.)

Lists 2,512 titles in classified order with author-subject index. Covers the history of Christianity in Western Europe, the Western Hemisphere, Eastern Europe and Western Asia, Africa, Asia and the islands of the Pacific. Brief descriptive or evaluative annotations are frequently given. While now old, it is still useful.

311. Chadwick, Owen. *The History of the Church; A Select Bibliography.* London: Historical Association, 1973. 52 pp.

First published 1962; revised and reprinted 1966, 1973. Annotated, classified; no index.

312. American Historical Association. *Guide to Historical Literature.* New York: The Macmillan Company, 1961. 962 pp.

Classified, annotated, prepared by specialists. Section on the history of religions includes subsection on Christianity, pp. 66–74.

313. Menendez, Albert J. *Church-State Relations: An Annotated Bibliography.* New York and London: Garland Publishing, Inc., 1976. 126 pp.

A classified bibliography that includes only full-length English-language books "which treat a subject in some depth or completeness" (Introduction). Doctoral dissertations, pamphlets, booklets, and periodical articles are excluded.

SURVEYS

314. Schaff, Philip. *History of the Christian Church.* New York: Charles Scribner's Sons, 1889–1910. 7 vols in 8.

A thorough, well-documented history of the church. Each volume has index of names and subjects.

315. ———. *The Creeds of Christendom; With a History and Critical Notes.* 6th ed., rev. and enl. New York and London: Harper & Brothers, 1919. (Bibliotheca Symbolica Ecclesiae Universalis.)

1st ed. 1877.

Vol. 1, The history of the creeds, including Ecumenical, Greek, Roman, Lutheran, Reformed, and Evangelical; Vol. 2, The Greek and Latin creeds, with translations; Vol. 3, The Evangelical Protestant creeds, with translations.

316. Latourette, Kenneth Scott. *A History of Christianity.* New York: Harper & Brothers, 1953. 1,516 pp.

A summary of the history of Christianity to the present, written as a new work and not as a condensation of his longer work, *A History of the Expansion of Christianity* (no. 485). Each chapter contains select bibliographies; detailed index included.

317. Walker, Williston. *A History of the Christian Church.* 3d ed., rev. by Robert T. Handy. New York: Charles Scribner's Sons, 1970. 601 pp.

1st ed., 1918; 2d ed., rev. by Cyril C. Richardson, Wilhelm Pauck, and Robert T. Handy, 1959.

The 2d edition provided a thorough revision of this popular, long-enduring survey written by a mature scholar. The 3d edition makes changes in the latter part of the book, adds a chapter, and updates the bibliography, pp. 561–584. Index included.

DICTIONARIES

318. *The Westminster Dictionary of Church History.* Jerald E. Brauer, ed. Philadelphia: The Westminster Press, 1971. 887 pp.

Provides brief, objective, unsigned articles on major persons, events, facts, and movements in the history of Christianity. Theological subjects are handled indirectly through biographical entries. Major emphasis is given to the modern period beginning with the eighteenth century, and to American church history. Brief bibliographies are appended to the longer articles.

See also *The Oxford Dictionary of the Christian Church* (no. 99), *Corpus Dictionary of Western Churches* (no. 100), and *The New International Dictionary of the Christian Church* (no. 101).

SOURCES

319. Kidd, Beresford James, ed. *Documents Illustrative of the History of the Church.* London: Society for Promoting Christian Knowledge; New York: The Macmillan Company, 1920–1941. 3 vols.

Vol. 1, to A.D. 313; Vol. 2, 313–461; Vol. 3, ca. 500–1500. Vols. 1 and 2 are now partially superseded by Stevenson (no. 320).

320. Stevenson, James, ed. *A New Eusebius: Documents Illustrative of the History of the Church to A.D. 337* . . . based upon the collection edited by the late B. J. Kidd. London: S.P.C.K., 1957. 427 pp.

Omits some of the sources in Kidd (no. 319), but adds others.

321. *The Library of Christian Classics.* John Baillie, John T. McNeill, Henry P. Van Dusen, eds. Philadelphia: The Westminster Press, 1953–1969. 26 vols.

A selection of works, usually with a new English translation, introductions, and notes, from the early church fathers through the end of the sixteenth century.

ATLAS

322. Littell, Franklin H. *The Macmillan Atlas History of Christianity.* New York: Macmillan Publishing Company, Inc.; London: Cassell & Collier Macmillan, 1976. 176 pp.

Rather than following primarily political or geographical boundaries, this atlas focuses on: (1) intellectual discipline (doctrine, dogmas, theology, confessions of faith); (2) moral and ethical disciplines (church discipline, social teachings, "Christianization" of society, internal style of life, relations with secular structures such as government); (3) expansion to a global religion from Palestinian beginnings (missions and ecumenics). Includes 197 maps, each of which is accompanied by text explaining "those times and places of crisis and decision—either internal or external or both— in which the shape and direction of the Christian movement was determined." (Foreword).

THE EARLY CHURCH

GUIDES AND MANUALS

323. Bardenhewer, Otto. *Patrology; The Lives and Works of the Fathers of the Church.* Translated from the 2d ed. by Thomas J. Shahan. Freiburg im Breisgau and St. Louis: Herder, 1908. 680 pp.

Includes biographical sketch, statement on writings and doctrine, and bibliography of works by and about each of the church fathers.

324. Quasten, Johannes. *Patrology.* Utrecht: Spectrum; Westminster, Md.: The Newman Press, 1950–1960. 3 vols.

An introduction intended for learners and specialists alike. Provides brief biographical sketches, summary of teachings, and excerpts from the writings of the church fathers. For each father there is a bibliography of critical editions, translations into modern languages, articles, and monographs. Special attention is given to sources and studies in English. This work is the basic guide in English.

BIBLIOGRAPHY

325. *Bibliographia Patristica. Internationale patristische Bibliographie.* 1956 to date. Berlin: Walter de Gruyter, 1959 to date. Annual.

Lists in classified order books and journal articles on the church fathers and related historical or theological topics. Author index appended. A separate section lists book reviews in alphabetical order by name of author of the book. International in coverage, ecumenical in authorship. No annotations.

326. *Bulletin de Théologie Ancienne et Médiévale.* 1929/1932 to date. Louvain: Abbaye du Mont César, 1929 to date. Quarterly.

Critical and detailed annotations on works appearing in patristics and medieval theology in many languages. International and ecumenical in coverage. Provides name index, doctrine index, and manuscript index. Issued as a supplement to *Recherches de Théologie Ancienne et Médiévale.*

DICTIONARIES

327. Smith, William, and Cheetham, Samuel, eds. *A Dictionary of Christian Antiquities;* being a continuation of the "Dictionary of the Bible." London: Murray; Hartford, Conn.: Burr, 1876–1880. 2 vols.

Covers the period from the time of the apostles to the age of Charlemagne (d. A.D. 814). Treats the organization of the church, its officers, legislation, discipline, and revenues; the social life of Christians, their worship and ceremonials, music, vestments, instruments, vessels, insignia, sacred places, architecture and art, symbolism, sacred days and seasons, graves and catacombs.

328. Smith, William, and Wace, Henry, eds. *A Dictionary of Christian Biography, Literature, Sects and Doctrines:* a continuation of "The Dictionary of the Bible." London: Murray; Boston: Little, 1877–1887. 4 vols.

Covers the period from the time of the apostles to the age of Charlemagne (d. A.D. 814). A companion work to *A Dictionary of Christian Antiquities* (no. 327). Treats all persons connected with the history of the church in the first eight centuries, the literature connected with them, and the controversies over doctrine or discipline in which they were engaged. Special attention is given to the church history of England, Scotland, and Ireland.

329. Wace, Henry, and Piercy, William C., eds. *A Dictionary of Christian Biography and Literature;* to the end of the sixth century A.D., with an account of the principal sects and heresies. London: Murray, 1911. 1,028 pp.

A one-volume abridgment and updating of the 4-vol. Smith and Wace work (no. 328). Does not supersede Smith and Wace, however, as this work omits longer articles and minor names and does not provide coverage beyond the sixth century.

SOURCES IN ENGLISH TRANSLATION

330. *The Ante-Nicene Fathers:* translations of the writings of the Fathers down to A.D. 325. Alexander Roberts and James Donaldson, eds. New York: Charles Scribner's Sons, 1899–1900. 10 vols. (Reprint: Grand Rapids, Mich.: Wm. B. Eerdmans Publishing Company, 1956.)

Contents: Vols. 1–8, Text; Vol. 9, Bibliographic synopsis; Vol. 10, Additional volume of text. Subject index in each volume and general index in Vol. 9. Contains numerous notes and Scripture references. Still a most basic collection.

331. *A Select Library of the Nicene and Post-Nicene Fathers of the Christian Church.* Philip Schaff, ed. New York: Christian Literature Co., 1887–1894. 14 vols.

————. ————. Second series. Philip Schaff and Henry Wace, eds. New York: Christian Literature Co., 1890–1900. 14 vols.

The first series includes writings of the fathers up to and including the principal works of Augustine and Chrysostom; the second series contains the chief works of the fathers from Eusebius to John of Damascus and from Ambrose to Gregory the Great.

332. *Ancient Christian Writers:* the works of the Fathers in translation. Johannes Quasten, Walter J. Burghardt, Thomas C. Lawler, eds. Westminster, Md., and New York: Newman Press, 1946 ff.

Some 40 volumes published thus far. The series aims at philological precision and theological understanding. An introduction, a new translation, extensive scholarly notes, and indexes included in each volume.

333. *The Fathers of the Church:* a new translation. Washington, D.C.: Catholic University of America, 1947 ff.

A less technical series than *Ancient Christian Writers* (no. 332); few footnotes, shorter introductions, brief index. One hundred volumes projected, with over two thirds now published.

334. Ayer, Joseph Cullen. *A Source Book for Ancient Church History;* from the apostolic age to the close of the conciliar period. New York: Charles Scribner's Sons, 1913. 707 pp.

Arranges selected illustrative sources by periods and then by subject within those periods. Provides citations where additional source materials may be found. Index included.

THE MEDIEVAL CHURCH

GUIDE

335. Paetow, Louis John. *A Guide to the Study of Medieval History.* Rev. ed. New York: F. S. Crofts & Co., 1931. 643 pp.

The standard guide for medieval studies. Classified order, annotations, complete index of authors, editors, subjects, and titles of large collections.

BIBLIOGRAPHY

336. Toronto University. St. Michael's College. Pontifical Institute of Medieval Studies. Library. *Dictionary Catalogue of the Library of the Pontifical Institute of Medieval Studies.* Boston: G. K. Hall & Company, 1972. 5 vols.

A photoreproduction, in book form, of the catalog of one of the outstanding North American library collections in medieval studies.

337. Rouse, Richard H. *Serial Bibliographies for Medieval Studies.* Berkeley and Los Angeles: University of California, 1969. 159 pp.

Lists and describes 283 bibliographies that cover current literature in medieval studies. Intended for beginning graduate students. Classified arrangement with index of titles and index of editors.

338. Atiya, Aziz S. *The Crusade: Historiography and Bibliography.* Bloomington: Indiana University Press, 1962. 170 pp.

Lists in classified order monographs, periodical literature, and collections of sources. Includes also a brief essay on the historiography of the Crusades. A scholarly work covering materials in several languages.

See also *Bulletin de Théologie Ancienne et Médiévale* (no. 326).

SURVEY

339. *The Cambridge Medieval History.* Cambridge: University Press, 1911–1936. 8 vols.

An authoritative work, written by specialists. Useful for reference purposes because of the full bibliographies at the end of each volume.

SOURCES IN ENGLISH TRANSLATION

340. Baldwin, Marshall W., ed. *Christianity Through the Thirteenth Century.* New York: Harper & Row, Publishers, Inc., 1970. 431 pp.

Contains documents illustrating Christian life, largely in the West, during four periods: the early Patristic age, the Carolingian age, the tenth through mid-twelfth centuries, and the High Middle Ages (1150–1300). Brief bibliographies accompany the various major sections. Index included.

REFORMATION AND COUNTER REFORMATION

BIBLIOGRAPHY

341. Bainton, Roland H., and Gritsch, Eric W. *Bibliography of the Continental Reformation:* Materials Available in English. 2d ed., rev. and enl. Hamden, Conn.: Archon Books, 1972. 220 pp.

Classified arrangement, brief annotations, no index. Covers Luther, Calvin, and related Reformers, the Anabaptists, Roman Catholic reform, Erasmus, and Arminius.

342. International Committee of Historical Sciences. Commission Internationale d'Histoire Ecclésiastique Comparée. *Bibliographie de la Réforme, 1450–1648.* Leiden: E. J. Brill, 1958–1970. 7 vols.

Lists monographs, journal articles, dissertations published

from 1940 to 1955 by country of origin and in alphabetical order within countries. Name index in each volume.

343. ———. ———. British Sub-Commission. *The Bibliography of the Reform, 1450–1648; Relating to the United Kingdom and Ireland for the Years 1955–1975.* Derek Baker, ed. Oxford: Basil Blackwell & Mott, Ltd., 1975. 242 pp.

Updates the above-listed work (no. 342) for England, Wales, Scotland, and Ireland. Includes books and parts of books, dictionaries and bibliographies, academic journals, society publications, reviews, completed theses. No index.

344. Archiv für Reformationsgeschichte. Archive for Reformation History. *Beiheft. Supplement. Literaturbericht. Literature Review.* Gütersloh: Gerd Mohn, 1972 to date.

An annual supplement to the journal of the same name (1903 to date); provides in classified order brief critical reviews of monographic and journal literature covering the Reformation in the period 1450–1650 in Western and Eastern Europe and Britain. Comprehensive subject coverage including religion, culture, state, science, philosophy, literature. Some reviews in English.

SURVEY

345. Grimm, Harold J. *The Reformation Era, 1500–1650.* 2d ed. New York: Macmillan Publishing Co., Inc., 1973. 594 pp.

A general survey with a detailed classified bibliography (pp. 509–580) that discusses both primary and secondary sources in various languages. Index included.

SOURCES IN ENGLISH TRANSLATION

346. Kidd, Beresford James, ed. *Documents Illustrating the Continental Reformation.* Oxford: Clarendon Press, 1911.

347. Hillerbrand, Hans J., ed. *The Protestant Reformation.* New York: Walker & Co., Inc., 1968. 290 pp. (Documentary History of Western Civilization.)

Contains selected writings from Luther, Zwingli, the Anabaptists, Calvin, and the English Reformation. The introductory essay lists various bibliographic aids, and the introductions to the documents provide additional bibliography.

THE MODERN CHURCH

BIBLIOGRAPHY

348. Roach, John. *A Bibliography of Modern History.* Cambridge: University Press, 1968. 388 pp.

Intended as a bibliographic supplement to *The New Cambridge Modern History* (no. 352). Divided into three sections covering the periods 1493–1648, 1648–1793, 1793–1945; arranged by subject within each period. Brief annotations. Manuscript sources and most periodical articles excluded. Main emphasis is on books in English and the better-known Western languages. Index of personal names (excluding authors) and of countries. Represents the work of over 170 scholars.

349. *Historical Abstracts.* Erich H. Boehm, ed. March 1955 to date. Santa Barbara, Calif.: Clio Press, 1955 to date. Quarterly.

Originally covered the period 1775–1945. Expanded with Vol. 17 and Vol. 19 to include 1450 to the present. Now Part A is "Modern Historical Abstracts, 1450–1914" and Part B is "Twentieth Century Abstracts, 1914–   ." Currently abstracts or cites from 2,000 serials published in eighty-five countries. All entries are in English, although original articles are published in thirty languages. Covers journals, serials, Festschriften, proceedings, and other collections. Includes both abstracts and short-entry citations. Includes the history of all countries except the United States and Canada, which is covered in *America: History and Life* (no. 367). Classified order with index in each issue; annual and five-year cumulated indexes also. Materials on church history included.

SURVEYS

350. Latourette, Kenneth Scott. *Christianity in a Revolutionary Age:* a history of Christianity in the nineteenth and twentieth centuries. New York: Harper & Brothers, 1958–1962. 5 vols.

A well-documented, thorough study of the life of the Roman Catholic, Protestant, and Eastern churches throughout the world from 1815 to the 1960's. Each volume has a briefly annotated bibliography and also a detailed index. Written by one of the twentieth century's most prolific church and missions historians.

351. *The Cambridge Modern History,* planned by the late Lord Acton, ed. by A. W. Ward (and others). Cambridge: University Press; New York: The Macmillan Company, 1902–1926. 13 vols. and atlas.

A still useful survey by specialists, with excellent bibliographies; extensive index in Vol. 13.

352. *The New Cambridge Modern History.* Cambridge: University Press, 1957–1970. 14 vols.

An updated version of the original work (no. 351), but less useful for reference purposes because it lacks bibliographies and footnotes. A bibliographic supplement, published separately, is available (no. 348).

THE BRITISH CHURCH

BIBLIOGRAPHY

The six works cited below are major bibliographic tools for British history. Each lists in classified order and then alphabetically under class: books, journal articles, collections of source materials, society proceedings, etc. Each work contains sections on church history.

353. Graves, Edgar B., ed. *A Bibliography of British History to 1485,* issued under the sponsorship of the Royal Historical Society, the American Historical Association, and the Mediaeval Academy of America. 2d ed. Oxford: University Press, 1974. 2 vols.

1st ed., 1901, ed. by Charles Gross.

Detailed table of contents and general index provided.

354. Read, Conyers. *Bibliography of British History: Tudor Period, 1485–1603,* issued under the direction of the American Historical Association and the Royal Historical Society of Great Britain. 2d ed. Oxford: Clarendon Press, 1959. 624 pp.

1st ed., 1933.

The 2d ed. has been strengthened, especially in the areas of Scottish, Welsh, Irish, and ecclesiastical history. Based on an exhaustive survey of the material in print up to January 1, 1957. Lists 6,543 entries; occasional brief annotations, prefatory notes for sections and subsections; detailed table of contents and author-subject index provided.

355. Davies, Godfrey, ed. *Bibliography of British History: Stuart Period, 1603–1714,* issued under the direction of the American Historical Association and the Royal Historical Society of Great Britain. 2d ed. Mary Frear Keeler, ed. Oxford: Clarendon Press, 1970. 734 pp.

1st ed., 1928.

Lists 4,350 works, usually with brief annotations and/or cross-references. Classified order with detailed table of contents and extensive main entry-subject index. Prefatory notes for sections and subsections.

356. Pargellis, Stanley, and Medley, D. J. *Bibliography of British History: The Eighteenth Century, 1714–1789,* issued under the direction of the American Historical Association and the Royal Historical Society of Great Britain. Oxford: Clarendon Press, 1951. 642 pp.

Includes 4,558 entries, with annotations and/or cross-references. Classified order, detailed table of contents and extensive main entry-subject index; greater emphasis on source literature than on secondary literature; journal literature excluded.

357. Brown, Lucy M., and Christie, Ian R. *Bibliography of British History, 1789-1851,* issued under the direction of the American Historical Association and the Royal Historical Society of Great Britain. Oxford: Clarendon Press, 1977. 759 pp.

Lists 4,782 entries, usually with brief annotations and some cross-references. Chapter on "Ecclesiastical History," pp.101-132. Main entry and subject index.

358. Hanham, H. J. *Bibliography of British History, 1851-1914,* issued under the direction of the American Historical Association and the Royal Historical Society of Great Britain. Oxford: Clarendon Press, 1976. 1,606 pp.

"The intention of this bibliography, as of the others in the series, is to list the major works which a student is likely to wish to consult, a selection of other works which makes clear the scope of contemporary printed materials, and a selection of biographies and bibliographies" (Preface). Chapter on "The Churches," pp. 387-463. Includes main entry and subject index.

LIBRARY CATALOGS

359. Williams Library, London. *Early Non-Conformity, 1566–1800; A Catalogue of Books in Dr. Williams's Library, London.* Boston: G. K. Hall & Co., 1968. 12 vols.

Offset reproduction of the card catalog. Vols. 1–5, Author catalog; Vols. 6–10, Subject catalog; Vols. 11–12, Chronological catalog.

The Williams Library was originally the library of Dr. Daniel Williams (ca. 1643–1717), a prominent Presbyterian minister first in Ireland and then in London. This book catalog consists "of the sheaf-catalogue of books in the Dr. Williams Library, printed in England between 1566 and 1800, together with related works from Scotland, Ireland, Wales and New England .... The Catalogue does not include books of purely devotional, catechetical or Biblical nature, nor the Library's numerous works by Continental reformers and Huguenot and Dutch theologians, except, as a general rule, where translated or published in England" (Preface). For description of the completed and updated catalog of the Williams Library, see no. 29.

360. New York (City). Union Theological Seminary. Library. *Catalogue of the McAlpin Collection of British History and Theology.* Compiled and edited by Charles Ripley Gillett. New York, 1927–1930. 5 vols.

Vols. 1–4, 1500–1700; Vol. 5, Index. Includes over 15,000 entries arranged chronologically and then alphabetically for each year; includes much pamphlet material as well as books. Vol. 5 provides a detailed index of authors and anonymous publications. An important source of British studies.

DICTIONARY

361. Ollard, Sidney Leslie; Cross, Gordon; and Bond, M. F. *Dictionary of English Church History.* 3d ed. rev. London: A. R. Mowbray & Co., Ltd.; New York: Morehouse-Gorham Company, Inc., 1948. 698 pp.

1st ed., 1912; 2d ed., 1919.

Scope limited strictly to the provinces of Canterbury and York. Bibliographies appended to most articles. Discusses history, doctrine, liturgy, ritual, vestments, architecture, controversies, etc. High church point of view.

SOURCES

362. Gee, Henry, and Hardy, William John. *Documents Illustrative of English Church History.* London: Macmillan, 1896. 607 pp.

A collection of primary sources, in English, from A.D. 314 to 1700. Arranged chronologically.

THE AMERICAN CHURCH

GUIDES AND MANUALS

363. U.S. Library of Congress. General Reference and Bibliographical Division. *A Guide to the Study of the United States of America;* representative books reflecting the development of American life and thought. Washington, D.C.: Library of Congress, 1960. 1,193 pp.

Includes a chapter on Religion, pp. 752–784. Detailed descriptive content annotations are provided for most works listed. Full author-title-subject index.

364. Freidel, Frank Burt, and Showman, Richard K. *Harvard Guide to American History.* Rev. ed. Cambridge: Belknap Press of Harvard University Press, 1974. 2 vols.

Vol. 1 arranged topically, emphasizing economic, social, and cultural history and biography. Vol. 2 in chronological order; chapter on Religion in Vol. 1, pp. 512–530. No annotations; extensive index of names and also a subject index. Monographic and journal literature, primary and secondary sources included.

BIBLIOGRAPHY

365. Burr, Nelson R. *A Critical Bibliography of Religion in America.* Princeton: Princeton University Press, 1961. 2 vols.

(Vol. 4 of *Religion in American Life,* ed. by James Ward Smith and A. Leland Jamison.)

A monumental work that provides a running account of American religious development and bibliographic information to document the narrative. Included are primary and secondary sources, monographs, journal articles, essays, and dissertations, all arranged in detailed classified order. Vol. 1 contains Part One, "Bibliographical Guides: General Surveys and Histories"; and Part Two, "Evolution of American Religion," which discusses the various denominations, sects, cults, and movements. Vol. 2 contains Part Three, "Religion and Society"; Part Four, "Religion in the Arts and Literature, Religion and the Arts"; and Part Five, "Intellectual History, Theology, Philosophy, and Science, American Theology." There is a detailed table of contents and author index. An indispensable tool for American religious studies.

366. Burr, Nelson R. *Religion in American Life.* New York: Appleton-Century-Crofts, 1971. 171 pp.

Classified order with very brief annotations and author index. Includes monographs, dissertations, and articles from theological, sociological, literary, scientific, and economic journals. Contains no running commentary as in *A Critical Bibliography of Religion in America* (no. 365).

367. *America: History and Life;* A guide to periodical literature. July 1964 to date. Santa Barbara, Calif.: Clio Press, 1964 to date. Quarterly.

Part A, Article abstracts and citations; Part B, Index to book reviews; Part C, American history bibliography (books, articles, dissertations); Part D, Annual index. Covers the history of the United States and Canada in works published throughout the world. Indexed annually and every five years. Includes materials on religious history.

SOURCES

368. Mode, Peter G. *Source Book and Bibliographical Guide for American Church History.* Menasha, Wisc.: Canta, 1921. 735 pp.

A collection of source documents from the seventeenth century through the early twentieth century illustrating the important developments in American church history. Eleven chapters are devoted to the various colonies, nine chapters to the various religious bodies, and the remaining chapters to special topics such as the Great Awakening, mission societies, westward expansion, work with the Indian and the Negro, the Civil War. Each chapter begins with a bibliographic essay discussing the primary and secondary sources relating to the subject of the chapter. Subject index included. While now old, this is still a most useful collection of sources.

369. Smith, H. Shelton; Handy, Robert T.; and Loetscher, Lefferts A. *American Christianity, An Historical Interpretation with Representative Documents.* New York: Charles Scribner's Sons, 1960, 1963. 2 vols.

Vol. 1, 1607–1820; Vol. 2, 1820–1960. Consists of approximately one third interpretative narrative and two thirds source documents illustrating the various periods and themes of American church history. Each chapter includes also an annotated bibliography and numerous footnotes. Vol. 1 contains 99 source documents; Vol. 2 contains 187; both provide concise table of contents and subject index.

370. Vaughan, Alden T., ed. *The Puritan Tradition in America, 1620–1730.* New York: Harper & Row, Publishers, Inc., 1972. 348 pp.

Documents arranged topically with brief introductions; concentrates on documents from Massachusetts Bay Colony.

371. Handy, Robert T., ed. *Religion in the American Experience: The Pluralistic Style.* Columbia, S.C.: University of South Carolina Press, 1972. 246 pp. (Documentary History of the United States, Harper Paperback edition, 1972.)

Illustrates American religious pluralism with documents reflecting various European traditions, tensions within American Protestantism, indigenous American churches, and the search for unity. Includes thirty-three source documents from the seventeenth century through the mid-twentieth century. Brief introductions to each document; emphasis on institutional life rather than theological thought.

372. Ahlstrom, Sydney E., ed. *Theology in America: The Major Protestant Voices from Puritanism to Neo-Orthodoxy.* In-

dianapolis: Bobbs-Merrill Company, Inc., 1967. 630 pp.

Contains selections from the writings of thirteen American religious leaders from Thomas Hooker (1586–1647) to H. Richard Niebuhr (1894–1962), with headnotes for each and a longer introductory essay setting forth the historical context of the American theological enterprise. Includes a selected bibliography, pp. 93–107, and an index.

Surveys

373. Ahlstrom, Sydney E. *A Religious History of the American People.* New Haven: Yale University Press, 1972. 1,158 pp.

A comprehensive survey that sets religious history in the larger frame of world history. Includes an extensive classified bibliography, pp. 1097–1128, and full index.

374. Hudson, Winthrop S. *Religion in America.* 2d ed. New York: Charles Scribner's Sons, 1973. 463 pp.

Provides equal coverage to the various periods from 1607 to the present. Bibliographic information on both primary and secondary sources included in the footnotes. Contains also a brief bibliography of paperback editions and a detailed index.

Denominations

Listed here are works dealing with both the history and the current status of the various mainline denominations and smaller church bodies in North America. For reference works by or about a specific denomination, see Chapter VII.

375. Sweet, William Warren. *Religion on the American Frontier;* a collection of source materials. New York: Harper & Brothers, 1931–1946. 4 vols. (Reprint: New York: Cooper Square Publishers, Inc., 1964.)

Vol. 1, Baptists, 1783–1830 (1931); Vol. 2, Presbyterians, 1783–1840 (1936); Vol. 3, Congregationalists, 1783–1850 (1939); Vol. 4, Methodists, 1783–1840 (1946). Each volume contains a lengthy general introduction, numerous documents arranged topically, extensive bibliography of manuscripts, official documents, printed sources, periodicals, and secondary materials, including books, articles, and pamphlets, and subject index.

376. *American Church History Series.* Philip Schaff, H. C. Potter, S. M. Jackson, gen. eds. New York: Christian Literature Co., 1893–1901. 13 vols.

A series of denominational histories by separate authors. Each volume contains a bibliography. Vol. 12 includes a bibliography of American church history, 1820–1893. Old, but still useful.

377. Mayer, Frederick W. *The Religious Bodies of America.* St. Louis, Mo.: Concordia Publishing House, 1954. 587 pp.

Provides scholarly discussion of the historical development and doctrine of Catholic, Lutheran, Reformed, Arminian, "Unionizing," "Inner Light," Millennial, Interdenominational, Anti-Trinitarian, Healing, and Esoteric religious bodies. Provides bibliography for each group; well-documented, full index; written from orthodox Lutheran perspective.

378. Mead, Frank S. *Handbook of Denominations in the United States.* 6th ed. Nashville: Abingdon Press, 1975. 320 pp.

Provides brief historical, doctrinal, and statistical information in narrative form on church bodies; arranged alphabetically. Includes list of headquarters of denominations, glossary of terms, bibliography, and index.

379. Rosten, Leo. *Religions of America; Ferment and Faith in an Age of Crisis;* a new guide and almanac. New York: Simon & Schuster, Inc., 1975. 672 pp.

Part One sets forth religious beliefs and credos of various church and even nonchurch groups in a direct question-and-answer form. Part Two is an almanac containing "a comprehensive collation of facts, events, opinion polls, statistics, analyses, and essays on the problems and crises confronting the churches today." Full index provided.

380. *Yearbook of American and Canadian Churches.* Constant H. Jacquet, Jr., ed. Prepared and edited in the Office of Research, Evaluation and Planning of the National Council of the Churches of Christ in the U.S.A. Nashville: Abingdon Press. 46th ed., 1978, 271 pp. Annual.

1st ed., 1916.

A useful compendium that "attempts to provide information on most of the established religious groups in the United States and Canada having the vast majority of membership but does not deal with most cults and sects" (Introduction). Also includes information on confessional bodies, ecumenical organizations, theological seminaries, religious periodicals, service agencies, church historical depositories, current and noncurrent membership, attendance, financial data, etc. Indexed.

BIOGRAPHY

For current biography of American religious leaders, see *Who's Who in Religion* (no. 527). For biography of clergymen to the year 1885 the following is still useful:

381. Sprague, William B. *Annals of the American Pulpit,* or commemorative notices of distinguished American clergymen of various denominations . . . . New York: Carter, 1855–1869. 9 vols.

Contains biographical and bibliographic information. Biographees are arranged by denomination and chronologically within denomination. No biographees were living at the time of publication. Where possible, testimony concerning the character of the biographee by a living contemporary is included.

ATLAS

382. Gaustad, Edwin Scott. *Historical Atlas of Religion in America.* Rev. ed. New York: Harper & Row, Publishers, Inc., 1976. 189 pp.

Shows the growth of both Colonial and non-Colonial denominations from 1650 to 1975 through the use of maps, charts, tables, and extensive texts. Provides indexes to authors and titles, to places, to religious bodies, to names and subjects.

CHAPTER VII

Denominational
Reference Works:
Catholic, Protestant, Jewish

Listed in this chapter are works by or about the Catholic Church, the various Protestant churches, and Judaism. Because of the close relationship between Christianity and Judaism, works on the latter are entered here rather than in the section on Comparative Religion in Chapter VIII. The works listed in this chapter cover the doctrine, history, polity, liturgy, ritual, and statistics of a particular religious body. For a survey or compendium of statistics or brief historical background of the various religious bodies of North America, see nos. 375–382.

CATHOLIC CHURCH

GUIDES AND MANUALS

383. *Guide to Catholic Literature, 1888–1940.* Detroit: Walter Romig & Company, 1940. 1,240 pp.

————, *1940–1967.* Ed. by Walter Romig. Grosse Pointe, Mich.: Walter Romig, Publisher, 1945–1968. Vols. 2–8.

A briefly annotated author-title-subject bibliography of books for adults, by or about Catholics. Merged with *Catholic Periodical Index* to form *Catholic Periodical and Literature Index* (nos. 386, 387).

384. Regis, Mary (Sister), ed. *The Catholic Bookman's Guide.* New York: Hawthorn Books, Inc., 1962. 638 pp.

An annotated, classified bibliography covering sources and evaluation, religion, philosophy, psychology, literature, and the social sciences. Includes primarily works in English. Represents the contribution of twenty-three specialists; provides complete author index and selected subject index.

See also McCabe (no. 17) and Steiner (no. 18).

LIBRARY CATALOG

385. *A Bibliography of the Catholic Church,* representing holdings of American libraries reported to the National Union Catalog in the Library of Congress. London and Chicago: Mansell Information/Publishing, Ltd., 1970. 572 pp. (Oversize.)

A reprint of material in Vols. 99–100 of the *National Union Catalog, Pre-1956 Imprints* (no. 30). Contains some 16,000 entries, and constitutes "one of the largest bibliographies in book form of publications of the various administrative, legislative and judicial organs of the Catholic Church and the largest listing of the official liturgical literature of the Church" (Foreword). Includes only works by the Catholic Church as "corporate author" and not works about the Catholic Church written by others. Locations in libraries in the United States and Canada of works listed are included with each entry.

INDEXES

386. *Catholic Periodical Index;* a cumulative author and subject index to a selected list of Catholic periodicals, 1930–1966. New York: The H. W. Wilson Company for the Catholic Library Association, 1939–1967. Quarterly, with biennial cumulations, Vols. 1–13.

Indexes 50–200 English-language Catholic periodicals published in North America and Great Britain. Merged with *Guide to Catholic Literature* (no. 383) to form the following:

387. *Catholic Periodical and Literature Index,* Vols. 14 ff., 1967/68 to date. Haverford, Pa.: Catholic Library Association, 1968 to date. Bimonthly, with biennial cumulations.

Indexes approximately 135 Catholic periodicals by author and subject and provides an annotated author-title-subject bibliography of adult books by Catholics or of Catholic interest. Papal documents, both text and commentary, in the original Latin and in translation in various languages are entered under the name of the pope in chronological order by date of issuance.

A separate section on book reviews is arranged alphabetically by the author of the book reviewed.

BIBLIOGRAPHY OF PAPAL PRONOUNCEMENTS

388. Carlen, Mary Claudia (Sister). *A Guide to the Encyclicals of the Roman Pontiffs from Leo XIII to the Present Day (1878–1937).* New York: The H. W. Wilson Company, 1939. 247 pp.

Lists general collections of encyclicals and individual encyclicals in the original Latin and in various translations, followed by citations for commentaries on the encyclicals. Includes a chronological index, Latin title index, and subject index.

389. ————. *Guide to the Documents of Pius XII, 1939–1949.* Westminster, Md.: Newman Press, 1951. 229 pp.

Carries forward the earlier guide (no. 388).

390. ————. *Dictionary of Papal Pronouncements, Leo XIII to Pius XII, 1878–1957.* New York: P. J. Kenedy & Sons, 1958. 216 pp.

Lists in alphabetical order by first word all encyclicals and a selection of other types of papal documents for the period designated. Provides a brief summary and cites sources in various languages for each document. Includes a chronological list of documents and a subject-title index.

BIBLIOGRAPHY AND SOURCES OF VATICAN II

391. Dollen, Charles. *Vatican II: A Bibliography.* Metuchen, N.J.: Scarecrow Press, 1969. 208 pp.

Lists about 2,500 English-language journal articles and books published 1959–1968; arranged in alphabetical order by author; includes subject index.

392. Vatican Council. 2d., 1962–1965. *The Documents of Vatican II,* in a new and definitive translation with commentaries and notes by Catholic, Protestant and Orthodox authorities. Walter M. Abbott, ed. New York: Herder & Herder, Inc., and Association Press, 1966. 793 pp.

Consists of an English translation of the sixteen Vatican II documents, each preceded with an introduction by a Catholic authority and followed by a response from a non-Catholic authority. Detailed topical index provided. An appendix contains an English translation of the text of Pope John's various messages before, during, and after the council.

393. Vatican Council. 2d., 1962–1965. *Vatican Council II, The Conciliar and Post-Conciliar Documents.* Austin Flannery, ed. Northport, N.Y.: Costello Publishing Co., Inc., 1975. 1,062 pp.

Contains an English translation of each of the sixteen Vatican II documents as well as 49 postconciliar documents related to them. An appendix lists 250 of the more important postconciliar documents, indicates which are present in this collection, and gives sources where all the originals may be found. An index of first words of the originals of the documents and a subject index are also included.

BIBLIOGRAPHY OF SPIRITUALITY

394. *Bibliographia Internationalis Spiritualitatis.* Edited by the Pontifical Institute of Spirituality. 1966 to date. Milan: Editrice Ancora, 1969 to date.

A comprehensive classified bibliography of monographic and journal literature on spirituality. Author index included.

BIBLIOGRAPHY OF CATHOLIC PHILOSOPHY

395. McLean, George Francis. *An Annotated Bibliography of Philosophy in Catholic Thought, 1900–1964.* New York: Frederick Ungar Publishing Company, 1967. 371 pp. (Philosophy in the 20th Century: Catholic and Christian, Vol. 1.)

Lists in classified order and annotates books for general readers, for students, and for scholars. Part I is arranged by subject areas and Part II by schools of Christian philosophy. Usually references are given to critical reviews for works listed. Author-title index included.

396. ————. *A Bibliography of Christian Philosophy and Contemporary Issues.* New York: Frederick Ungar Publishing Company, 1967. 312 pp. (Philosophy in the 20th Century: Catholic and Christian, Vol. 2.)

Lists books and journal articles in classified order. An appendix lists doctoral dissertations in philosophy submitted to Catholic universities in North America. Author index included.

BIBLIOGRAPHY, SOURCES, AND SURVEY
OF THE CATHOLIC CHURCH IN THE UNITED STATES

397. Vollmar, Edward J. *The Catholic Church in America: An Historical Bibliography.* 2d ed. New York: Scarecrow Press, 1963. 399 pp.

Lists alphabetically by author books, pamphlets, and journal articles written 1850–1950; also primary and secondary sources. No annotations. Included are titles of unpublished doctoral dissertations and master's theses submitted to degree-granting Catholic colleges. Subject index provided.

398. Ellis, John Tracy. *A Guide to American Catholic History.* Milwaukee: Bruce Publishing Company, 1959. 147 pp.

A classified, critically annotated bibliography of 814 entries covering primary and secondary sources, including doctoral dissertations and master's theses. Separate chapters devoted to diocesan, sectional, and parish history; biography; religious communities; education; and special studies such as colonization, journalism, legal studies, missions, nationalities, nativism, social studies, war and international relations. Author, title, and subject index.

399. ———. *Documents of American Catholic History.* 3d ed. Chicago: Henry Regnery Co., 1967. 2 vols.

Vol. 1, The Church in the Spanish colonies to the Second Plenary Council at Baltimore in 1866. Vol. 2, From the Second Plenary Council at Baltimore in 1866 to the present.

400. ———. *American Catholicism.* 2d ed., rev. Chicago: The University of Chicago Press, 1969. 322 pp. (The Chicago History of American Civilization.)

A brief survey with bibliographic notes, important dates, and suggested reading. Subject index included.

401. Cadden, John Paul. *The Historiography of the American Catholic Church, 1785–1943.* Washington, D.C.: Catholic University of America Press, 1944. 122 pp. (Catholic University of America Studies in Sacred Theology, No. 82.)

Submitted as a doctoral dissertation. Includes main entry index.

BIBLIOGRAPHY OF CANON LAW

402. *Canon Law Abstracts:* a half-yearly review of periodical literature in canon law. Melrose, Scotland: Canon Law Society of Great Britain, 1958 to date. Semiannual.

International in scope. Includes current as well as historical subjects. Indexes articles and case reports.

ENCYCLOPEDIAS

403. *Catholic Encyclopedia;* an international work of reference on the constitution, doctrine, discipline and history of the Catholic Church. New York: Catholic Encyclopedia Press, 1907–1922. 17 vols.

The older, comprehensive, authoritative English-language work on Catholic history, doctrine, ritual, etc. Written from a pre-Vatican II perspective. While now old, still a useful work in the areas of philosophy, art, medieval literature, history. Vol. 16 contains additional articles and index; Vol. 17, Supplement.

404. *New Catholic Encyclopedia.* Prepared by an Editorial Staff at The Catholic University of America, Washington, D.C. New York: McGraw-Hill Book Co., Inc., 1967. 16 vols.

An entirely new work and not a revision of the *Catholic Encyclopedia* (no. 403). Reflects the broader outlook of Vatican II. Emphasis is on the Catholic Church in the United States and the English-speaking world, but the work is international and ecumenical in scope. Special attention is given to the church in Latin America. Selective bibliographies, appended to nearly all articles, are most useful. Vol. 16 is the index.

DICTIONARIES

405. Addis, William E., and Arnold, Thomas. *A Catholic Dictionary.* Rev. by T. B. Scannel; further rev. with additions by P. E. Hallett. 17th ed. London: Routledge & Kegan Paul, Ltd., 1960. 860 pp.

1st ed. 1886.

Longer, more scholarly articles. No bibliography, but some footnotes. No biography.

406. *A Catholic Dictionary* (The Catholic Encyclopaedic Dictionary). Donald Attwater, ed. 3d ed. New York: The Macmillan Company, 1958. 552 pp.

A popular work designed "with particular regard to the requirements of Catholic lay-people and with the hope of being useful to non-Catholic journalists and general enquirers" (Preface). Short articles, no bibliography, no biography. More detailed information on the church in Great Britain and Ireland and, to a lesser extent, the United States.

407. *The Maryknoll Catholic Dictionary.* Albert J. Nevins, ed. New York: Grossett & Dunlap, Inc., 1965. 710 pp.

Produced by the Catholic Foreign Mission Society of America, the Maryknoll Fathers, this work reflects the many changes in liturgy, discipline, and organization of the Catholic Church since Vatican II. It is intended for the general reader in the United States and Canada. Provides good coverage for the church's missionary enterprise and for Biblical subjects. Useful appendixes on Catholic abbreviations and Catholic forms of address; information on saints, popes, prominent deceased North American Catholics, American martyrs, and international Catholic organizations. No bibliography.

Yearbooks and Almanacs

408. *Annuario Pontificio.* Vatican City: Libreria Editrice Vaticana. Annual.

The official universal yearbook of the Catholic Church. Well indexed.

409. *The Official Catholic Directory . . .* containing ecclesiastical statistics of the United States, the Canal Zone, Puerto Rico, the Virgin Islands, Agana, Carolina and Marshall Islands, foreign missionary activities, Canada, and Mexico. New York: P. J. Kenedy & Sons. Annual.

The basic statistical source for the Catholic Church in the United States. Lists name of every priest, church, institution.

Briefer statistics provided for other places mentioned in the subtitle.

410. *Catholic Almanac.* Huntington, Ind.: Our Sunday Visitor, 1904 to date. Annual.

Previously titled *St. Anthony's Almanac,* produced by different publishers in various places. Contains facts and statistics on current events, special reports on current issues, information on the church hierarchy, doctrine, liturgy, sacraments, calendar, saints, biography, missions, education, social services, orders, publishing, etc. Well indexed.

BIOGRAPHY

411. Delaney, John J., and Tobin, James Edward. *Dictionary of Catholic Biography.* Garden City, N.J.: Doubleday & Company, Inc., 1961. 1,245 pp.

Contains almost 15,000 biographical sketches of "outstanding Catholics from the time of the Apostles to the present day" (Foreword). No living persons are included. Bibliographic references given only for major figures.

412. *The American Catholic Who's Who.* 1934/35 to date. Detroit: Walter Romig & Company, 1935 to date. Biennial.

Vol. 21 (1976–1977) published in Washington by the National Catholic News Service. Contains brief biographical sketches giving profession, parentage, education, positions held, writings, etc.

SAINTS

A most useful guide to the vast literature on the lives of the saints may be found in McCabe (no. 17), pp. 62–68. Here will be listed only a single ready-reference tool.

413. *The Book of the Saints:* a dictionary of persons canonized or beatified by the Catholic Church. Compiled by the Benedictine Monks of St. Augustine's Abbey, Ramsgate. 5th ed. New York: Thomas Y. Crowell Co., 1966. 740 pp.

1st ed., 1921.

The scope and accuracy of this work has been improved with each succeeding edition. A most useful one-volume work.

PROTESTANT CHURCHES

Cited in this section are substantial reference or bibliographic tools related to a particular Protestant church or confessional family. Omitted because of the lack of space are the official yearbooks, minutes, reports, hymnals, or worship books issued by most denominations. Works are grouped by denominational or confessional family listed in alphabetical order.

BAPTIST

414. Starr, Edward Caryl. *A Baptist Bibliography:* being a register of printed material by and about Baptists; including works written against the Baptists. Rochester, N.Y.: American Baptist Historical Society, 1947–1976. 25 vols.

An alphabetical unannotated listing of works published from 1609 to the present, with locations given. Location symbols for libraries in the United States and Canada explained only in Vol. 1. Each volume contains an index to joint authors, translators, Baptist publishers, distinctive titles, and subjects. A monumental work.

415. Gill, Athol. *A Bibliography of Baptist Writings on Baptism, 1900–1968.* Rüschlikon-Zürich: Baptist Theological Seminary, 1969. 184 pp.

Comprehensive, classified, international in scope. Includes books, articles, book reviews. Provides an index of authors, an index of authors of books reviewed, and a list of Baptist periodicals.

416. *Encyclopedia of Southern Baptists.* Nashville: The Broadman Press, 1958. 2 vols.

————. Supplement. Vol. 3. 1971.

Signed articles with bibliography. Biographies also included. About 20 percent of the articles deal with general background, while the remainder deal with Southern Baptist organizations, institutions, agencies, and personalities.

417. *Southern Baptist Periodical Index.* Nashville: Historical Commission of the Southern Baptist Convention, 1965 to date. Annual.

Author-subject index now covering forty-six periodicals published by sixteen Southern Baptist agencies. Beginning in 1975 the index was produced by the Baptist Information Retrieval System (BIRS), a centralized computer system.

BRETHREN

418. Durnbaugh, Donald F., and Shultz, Lawrence W. "A Brethren Bibliography, 1713–1963; Two Hundred Fifty Years of Brethren Literature," in *Brethren Life and Thought,* Vol. 9, Nos. 1 and 2 (Winter and Spring, 1964). 177 pp.

Attempts to list all publications of Brethren authors issued prior to 1900 and selectively after 1900. "Authors belonging to all those bodies which look to the Schwarzenau Brethren as their progenitors have been included, as far as obtainable" (Introduction). Arranged chronologically and alphabetically by author within each year; brief annotations. Index of authors, editors, and compilers. Locations given.

CONGREGATIONAL *(See also United Church of Christ)*

419. Dexter, Henry Martyn. *The Congregationalism of the Last Three Hundred Years, as Seen in Its Literature.* New York: Harper, 1880. 716 pp. Bibliographical appendix, 326 pp.

Consists of twelve well-documented lectures and an extensive bibliography entitled "Collections toward a bibliography of Congregationalism," arranged in chronological order by year, and alphabetically within a given year, with locations cited.

420. Walker, Williston. *The Creeds and Platforms of Congregationalism,* with an introduction by Douglas Horton. Boston: Pilgrim Press, 1960. 604 pp.

First published by Scribner, 1893. Contains primary source documents of Congregationalism from 1582 to 1883. Introductions and bibliography accompany each chapter; detailed index provided.

421. Peel, Albert. *The Congregational Two Hundred, 1530–1948.* London: Independent Press, Ltd., 1948. 288 pp.

Contains biographical sketches and brief bibliography for two hundred leading British and American Congregationalists.

DISCIPLES OF CHRIST

422. Spencer, Claude E. *An Author Catalog of Disciples of Christ and Related Religious Groups.* Canton, Mo.: Disciples of Christ Historical Society, 1946. 367 pp.

Lists in alphabetical order by author both religious and secular books and pamphlets by members of the Disciples of Christ, the Christian Church, and the Churches of Christ. Author's place and date of birth and date of death given, when known. No subject index.

423. ———. *Theses Concerning the Disciples of Christ and Related Religious Groups.* 2d ed. Nashville: Disciples of Christ Historical Society, 1964. 94 pp.

1st ed., 1941.

Lists 743 dissertations and theses from eighty-nine institutions alphabetically by author. Subject index and institution index included.

HOLINESS DENOMINATIONS

424. Jones, Charles Edwin. *A Guide to the Study of the Holiness Movement.* Metuchen, N.J.: Scarecrow Press and the American Theological Library Association, 1974. 918 pp. (American Theological Library Association Bibliography Series, No. 1.)

A comprehensive bibliography of the denominations and associations of the American Holiness and Holiness-Pentecostal movement. Includes their publications, schools, missions, leaders, doctrine, worship, and history. Detailed author-subject index provided.

425. Dayton, Donald W. *The American Holiness Movement; A Bibliographic Introduction.* Wilmore, Ky.: B. L. Fisher Library, Asbury Theological Seminary, 1971. 59 pp.

A bibliographic essay that first appeared in the 1971 *Proceedings* of the American Theological Library Association. Covers the bibliography, history, biography, theology, periodicals, missions, hymnody, preaching, historical collections, and recent trends of the American Holiness movement.

LUTHERAN

426. Bodensieck, Julius, ed. *The Encyclopedia of the Lutheran Church.* Edited for the Lutheran World Federation. Minneapolis: Augsburg Publishing House, 1965. 3 vols.

The most comprehensive encyclopedia of the Lutheran Church. International and ecumenical in scope. Longer, signed articles, with bibliographies, covering Bible, doctrine, ethics, philosophy, church history, polity, Christian education, practical theology, ecumenical relations, and biography. The historical and theological articles are often substantial treatises. The article on "Bible," for example, is 92 pages, with the subsection on "Bible Versions" running 36 pages.

427. *Lutheran Cyclopedia.* Erwin L. Lueker, ed. St. Louis: Concordia Publishing House, 1975. 845 pp.

1st ed., 1954.

A general religious encyclopedia, not limited in scope only to the Lutheran Church; shorter articles, some with bibliography; strong in Lutheran biography, although no living persons are included.

MENNONITES, ANABAPTISTS, AND THE RADICAL REFORMATION

428. Hillerbrand, Hans Joachim. *A Bibliography of Anabaptism, 1520–1630.* Elkhart, Ind.: Institute of Mennonite Studies, 1962. 281 pp.

Under the main headings of areas, persons, and topical studies, lists in chronological order primary and secondary works, monographic and journal literature. Locations, mostly in North American libraries, indicated for monographic entries published before 1940. Includes title index and author index.

429. Springer, Nelson P., and Klassen, A. J. *Mennonite Bibliography, 1631-1961.* Compiled . . . under the direction of the Institute of Mennonite Studies. Scottdale, Pa., and Kitchener, Ont.: Herald Press, 1977. 2 vols. 531 and 634 pp.

Contents: Vol. 1, International, Europe, Latin America, Asia, Africa; Vol. 2, North America, Indexes.

A massive work of scholarship that continues Hillerbrand's work (no. 428). Includes periodicals, books, pamphlets, dissertations, Festschriften, symposia, and periodical and encyclopedia articles. Locations in North American and European libraries indicated. Arranged geographically, topically within areas, and then chronologically and alphabetically within topics. Includes author, subject, and book review indexes.

430. Bender, Harold S. *Two Centuries of American Mennonite Literature;* a bibliography of Mennonitica Americana, 1727–1928. Goshen, Ind.: Mennonite Historical Society, 1929. 181 pp. (Studies in Anabaptist and Mennonite History, 1.)

"The purpose of this bibliography is to present as completely as possible a list of all the books, pamphlets, and periodicals, including reprints, by Mennonites in the United States and Canada from the time of the first settlement until the end of the year 1928" (Preface). Literature of each of the three main Mennonite church groups is arranged chronologically and then alphabetically by main entry within each year. Author index and title index.

431. Hostetler, John A. *Annotated Bibliography on the Amish;* an annotated bibliography of source materials pertaining to the Old Order Amish Mennonites. Scottdale, Pa.: Mennonite Publishing House, 1951. 100 pp.

Lists in alphabetical order by author in four separate sections: books and pamphlets, graduate theses, articles, unpublished sources. Analytical subject index.

432. Epp, Frank H. *Mennonites in Canada, 1786–1920;* the history of a separate people. Toronto: The Macmillan Co. of Canada, Ltd., 1974. 480 pp.

A historical survey with extensive bibliographies, pp. 419–473. Indexed.

433. *The Mennonite Encyclopedia;* a comprehensive reference work on the Anabaptist-Mennonite movement. Hillsboro, Kans.: Mennonite Brethren Publishing House; Newton, Kans.: Mennonite Publication Office; Scottdale, Pa.: Mennonite Publishing House, 1955–1959. 4 vols. and index.

Designed "to give comprehensive and authentic information on a wide range of historical and contemporary topics related to the Anabaptist-Mennonite movement from the beginning in the early 16th century to the present time" (Preface). Contains longer, signed articles with bibliographies as well as brief articles on over 2,000 known Anabaptist martyrs—Swiss, German, and Dutch. Much of the European material is based on the *Mennonitisches Lexikon* (1913–1967, 4 vols.); provides extensive coverage of North and South American Mennonitism.

METHODIST

434. Rowe, Kenneth E., ed. *Methodist Union Catalog; Pre-1956 Imprints.* Vols I-III (A-Dix) ff. Metuchen, N.J.: Scarecrow Press, 1975 ff.

When completed, this work will "constitute the most comprehensive bibliography in book form of publications by and about the people called Methodists since their beginnings at Oxford in 1729 to the present around the world" (Introduction). Includes books, pamphlets, and theses on Methodist history, biography, doctrine, polity, missions, education, and sermons. Manuscripts, periodicals, and other serials excluded. Locations of copies in over 200 libraries in North America and Europe are indicated. Arranged alphabetically by author. Indexes by subject, title, and added entries are planned.

435. *Methodist Union Catalog of History, Biography, Disciplines and Hymnals;* preliminary edition. Brook Bivens Little, ed. Lake Junaluska, N.C.: Association of Methodist Historical Societies, Upper Room Devotional Library, Methodist Librarians' Fellowship, 1967. 478 pp.

Will be superseded by the previously listed work (no. 434) when that is completed. Lists in alphabetical order, by main entry, works held in sixteen Methodist libraries in the United States. Consists of photocopied shelf list cards from the participating libraries.

436. *The Encyclopedia of World Methodism;* sponsored by the World Methodist Council and the Commission on Archives and History of the United Methodist Church. Nolan B. Harmon, ed. Nashville: United Methodist Publishing House, 1974. 2 vols.

Contains numerous biographies, including living persons, as well as articles on Methodist history, sites, doctrine, institutions, congregations, conferences, statistics; strong emphasis on the United Methodist Church and American Methodism. Signed articles with bibliographies. General index provided in the appendix.

437. Batsel, John D., and Batsel, Lyda K. *Union List of United Methodist Serials, 1773-1973.* Evanston, Ill.: Commission on Archives and History of the United Methodist Church, the United Methodist Librarians' Fellowship, and Garrett Theological Seminary, 1974. 136 pp.

Provides bibliographic and holdings information for Methodist and Evangelical United Brethren serials in over one hundred libraries in the United States.

438. *United Methodist Periodical Index.* Nashville, Tenn.: United Methodist Publishing House, 1961 to date. Quarterly, with annual and five-year cumulations.

An author-subject index of selected United Methodist periodicals.

439. *Who's Who in the Methodist Church.* Compiled by the Editors of Who's Who in America and the A. N. Marquis Company, Inc., with the cooperation of the Council of Secretaries of the Methodist Church. Nashville and New York: Abingdon Press, 1966. 1,489 pp.

Brief biographical sketches with home and office addresses of biographee.

440. McIntosh, Lawrence D. "The Place of John Wesley in the Christian Tradition; A Selected Bibliography," pp. 134-159 in *The Place of Wesley in the Christian Tradition;* essays delivered at Drew University in celebration of the commencement of the publication of the Oxford Edition of the *Works* of John Wesley. Kenneth E. Rowe, ed. Metuchen, N.J.: Scarecrow Press, 1976.

Classified arrangement of materials dealing with Wesley and eighteenth-century British Methodism.

441. Melton, J. Gordon. *A (First Working) Bibliography of Black Methodism.* Evanston, Ill.: Institute for the Study of American Religion, 1970. 45 pp. (Bibliographic Monograph No. 1.)

Lists by denomination or church agency books by and about black Methodists. Some theses, periodicals, and pamphlets are

included when these highlight an otherwise neglected aspect.
Some locations given.

See also Sweet (no. 375), Vol. 4.

MORMON

442. Brigham Young University, Provo, Utah. College of
Religious Instruction. *A Catalogue of Theses and Dissertations
Concerning the Church of Jesus Christ of Latter-Day Saints,
Mormonism and Utah;* completed to January 1970. Provo,
Utah, 1971. 742 pp.

443. Brooks, Melvin R. *Latter-Day Saints Reference Encyclopedia.* Salt Lake City: Bookcraft, 1960. 541 pp.

444. *Index to Periodicals of the Church of Jesus Christ of
Latter-Day Saints.* Salt Lake City, Utah: The Church of Jesus
Christ of Latter-Day Saints, 1961 to date.

Annual author-subject index to five official Latter-Day Saints
periodicals.

PLYMOUTH BRETHREN

445. Ehlert, Arnold D. *Brethren Writers:* a checklist with an
introduction to Brethren literature and additional lists. Grand
Rapids, Mich.: Baker Book House, 1969. 83 pp.

Discusses Plymouth Brethren literature, authors, editors,
translators, periodicals, publishers, initials, and pseudonyms.

PRESBYTERIAN

446. Trinterud, Leonard J. *A Bibliography of American Presbyterianism During the Colonial Period.* Philadelphia: The Presbyterian Historical Society, 1968. No paging.

Lists 1,129 primary source documents from twelve Colonial
presbyteries or synods and indicates their locations in libraries.
Author index.

447. Armstrong, Maurice W.; Loetscher, Lefferts A.; and
Anderson, Charles A. *The Presbyterian Enterprise;* sources of
American Presbyterian history. Philadelphia: The Westminster
Press, 1956. 336 pp.

Contains letters, journals, diaries, periodicals, minutes, and other documents illustrating the history of American Presbyterianism from 1706 to 1956. An appendix of documents quoted and an author-subject index are included.

See also Sweet (no. 375), Vol. 2.

SEVENTH-DAY ADVENTIST

448. *Seventh-Day Adventist Encyclopedia.* Washington, D.C.: Review and Herald Publishing Association, 1966. 1,452 pp. (Commentary Reference Series, Vol. 10.)

A comprehensive compendium on the history, organization, operation, institutions, beliefs, practices, and leaders of the Seventh-Day Adventist Church. No bibliography.

449. *Seventh-Day Adventist Periodical Index.* Riverside, Calif.: Loma Linda University Libraries, 1971 to date. Semi-annual.

Author-subject index to some forty-eight Seventh-Day Adventist publications.

UNITED CHURCH OF CHRIST *(See also Congregational)*

The Congregational Christian Churches and the Evangelical and Reformed Church merged in 1957 to form the United Church of Christ.

450. Keiling, Hans Peter. *The Formation of the United Church of Christ (U.S.A.):* a bibliography. Pittsburgh: The Clifford E. Barbour Library, Pittsburgh Theological Seminary, 1970. No paging.

Lists in classified order 1,655 items, 90 percent of which are primary sources relating to the formation of the United Church of Christ. Includes denominational records, committee minutes, individual statements or letters, pro and con merger pamphlets, court records, books, journal and newspaper articles, interviews; originally part of a doctoral dissertation. Index of persons.

JUDAISM

BIBLIOGRAPHY

451. Shunami, Shlomo. *Bibliography of Jewish Bibliographies.* Photographic reprint of "Second Edition Enlarged," 1965, with corrections. Jerusalem: Magnes, Hebrew University, 1969. 997 pp.

1st ed., 1936.

Contains 4,727 entries, some with very brief annotations, arranged in classified order. Comprehensive, international. Lists bibliographies in Hebrew as well as in many other languages. Covers Hebrew religion, literature, sociology, science, Zionism, Palestine, history, the Holocaust, Hebrew typography, manuscripts, etc. Provides index of Hebrew titles, index of names and subjects.

452. *The Study of Judaism:* bibliographical essays. New York: Anti-Defamation League of B'nai B'rith, 1972. 229 pp.

Consists of six bibliographic essays by specialists on both ancient and modern Judaism.

453. Berlin, Charles. *Index to Festschriften in Jewish Studies.* Cambridge, Mass.: Harvard College Library; New York: Ktav Publishing House, Inc., 1971. 319 pp.

Indexes 243 Festschriften consisting of 259 volumes by an author index and a subject index. The Festschriften indexed are listed alphabetically by the name of the person being honored or memorialized.

454. Celnik, Max, and Celnik, Isaac. *Bibliography on Judaism and Jewish-Christian Relations.* New York: Anti-Defamation League of B'nai B'rith, 5725 (1965). 68 pp.

Lists in classified order almost 300 works by Jewish authors about Judaism and Jewish life. Intended for the generalist: writers and editors of Christian education textbooks, faculty and students of theological seminaries, clergy and laity. Author-title index included.

ENCYCLOPEDIAS AND DICTIONARIES

455. *Encyclopedia Judaica.* Jerusalem: Encyclopedia Judaica Jerusalem; New York: The Macmillan Company, 1971. 16 vols.

Up-to-date, scholarly, comprehensive. Contains longer, signed articles with bibliographies; considerable biographical information; well illustrated. Index is in Vol. 1. Represents an entirely new undertaking as well as the completion of a work in German with the same title (1928–1934) that suspended publication after the letter "L" (Vol. 10). This work is the first source to consult on Jewish subjects.

456. *The Universal Jewish Encyclopedia.* Isaac Landman, ed. New York: The Universal Jewish Encyclopedia, Inc., 1939–1943. 10 vols.

————. Reading guide and index. 1944. 78 pp.

A popular, nonscholarly work, emphasizing American Jewish life and twentieth-century Jewish biography.

457. *The Jewish Encyclopedia.* Isidore Singer, ed. New York and London: Funk & Wagnalls, 1903–1906. 12 vols.

The first major English-language encyclopedia of this nature. A monumental work for its time, although it tends to overlook Eastern European Jewry, Kabbalah and Hasidism, Yiddish language and literature, and the Jews in Moslem lands. Superseded by *Encyclopedia Judaica* (no. 455), although still useful for biography and historical information.

458. *The Standard Jewish Encyclopedia.* Cecil Roth, ed. Garden City, N.Y.: Doubleday & Company, Inc., 1959. 1,978 pp.

A useful, well-illustrated one-volume reference tool with strong emphasis on recent developments in Jewish life, the American Jewish community, biographical information, and the state of Israel. The editor served also as the editor of the *Encyclopedia Judaica* (no. 455) until his death in 1970.

459. Werblowsky, R. J. Zwi, and Wigoder, Geoffrey, eds. *The Encyclopedia of the Jewish Religion.* New York: Holt, Rinehart & Winston, 1966 (Copr. 1965). 415 pp.

Intended to provide "the interested layman with concise, accurate, and non-technical information on Jewish belief and practices, religious movements and doctrines as well as the names and concepts that have played a role in Jewish religious history" (Preface). Does not cover Jewish culture, history, or biography.

460. Isaacson, Ben, and Wigoder, Deborah. *The International Jewish Encyclopedia.* Jerusalem: Massada Press; Engle-

wood Cliffs, N.J.: Prentice-Hall, Inc., 1973. 336 pp.

A popularly written one-volume work intended primarily for young people; covers religion, history, literature, and culture of Judaism, but emphasizes events of the past thirty years. No bibliography; index included.

PERIODICAL INDEX

461. *Index to Jewish Periodicals;* an author and subject index to selected English-language journals of general and scholarly interest. Cleveland Heights, Ohio: Index to Jewish Periodicals, 1963 to date. Semiannual with annual cumulation.

Indexes over forty journals, most of which are published in the United States and Great Britain.

CHAPTER VIII

Practical Theology, Missions, Ecumenics, and Comparative Religion

PRACTICAL THEOLOGY

The brevity of this section compared to others, such as Biblical materials (nos. 127–287) or church history (nos. 310–382), indicates the paucity of reference and bibliographic tools in English in practical theology. In addition to the works listed here, the *Index to Religious Periodical Literature* (no. 43) under the appropriate subject headings is a most useful tool in this area.

HOMILETICS

462. Toohey, William, and Thompson, William D., eds. *Recent Homiletical Thought, A Bibliography, 1935–1965*. Nashville and New York: Abingdon Press, 1967. 303 pp.

Conceived by officers of the Catholic Homiletic Society, but carried out on an ecumenical basis with thirty-four contributors, this work lists in classified order and annotates 2,137 books, journal articles, theses, and dissertations. Author index provided. Indication of Catholic or Protestant authorship, when known, is given for the 446 books listed.

LITURGY

463. Vismans, Th. A., and Brinkhoff, Lucas. *Critical Bibliography of Liturgical Literature*. English edition translated from German by Raymund D. Fitzpatrick and Clifford Howell. Nijmegen: Bestelcentrale der V.S.K.B. (Dutch Association of Seminary and Monastery Librarians), 1961. 72 pp.

A classified listing with annotations of 278 liturgical sources, commentaries, handbooks, monographs, and periodicals. Mostly Catholic, but a brief section on Eastern and Protestant liturgy is included. Index of authors and anonymous works provided.

464. Podhradsky, Gerhard. *New Dictionary of the Liturgy.* London: Geoffrey Chapman, Ltd., 1967. 208 pp.

Original German edition, 1962.

New material added to the English edition. Provides brief, succinct articles with historical and theological background on the Roman Catholic liturgy in the light of Vatican II. Illustrations and general bibliography included.

465. Davies, J. G., ed. *A Dictionary of Liturgy and Worship.* New York: Macmillan Publishing Co., Inc., 1972. 385 pp.

An ecumenically oriented work with over sixty contributors from the various confessional bodies. Signed articles, some of them long (e.g., "Baptism," pp. 44–64), most with bibliography. Includes cross-references and illustrations.

HYMNOLOGY

466. Julian, John, ed. *A Dictionary of Hymnology,* setting forth the origin and history of Christian hymns of all ages and nations. Rev. ed., with a new supplement. London: Murray; New York: Charles Scribner's Sons, 1907. 1,768 pp. (Reprint: New York: Dover Publications, Inc., 1957.)

While now old, still the most comprehensive work in English covering the historical, biographical, doctrinal, devotional, and liturgical aspects of hymnology. Covers hymns of all languages and nations, but concentrates on hymns in hymnals of the English-speaking countries. Includes indexes of first lines, of authors and translators.

467. Diehl, Katherine Smith. *Hymns and Tunes: An Index.* New York and London: Scarecrow Press, 1966. 1,185 pp.

Indexes the hymns from seventy-eight English-language hymnals by first lines and variants, authors and first lines, tune names and variants, composers and tune names, and melodies. Indicates by symbols in which hymnals the hymns indexed may be found.

468. McDormand, Thomas B., and Crossman, Frederic S.

Judson Concordance to Hymns. Valley Forge, Pa.: Judson Press, 1965. 375 pp.

Provides a concordance to key words in 2,342 hymns which are identified by first line. Useful for discovering the title of a hymn when only a phrase from one of its stanzas is known. Should be used in conjunction with Diehl (no. 467) for identifying the hymnal that contains a particular hymn.

469. McCutchan, Robert Guy. *Hymn Tune Names, Their Sources and Significance.* New York and Nashville: Abingdon Press, 1957. 206 pp.

Consists mainly of an alphabetical list of names of tunes with their melodies, meter markings, first phrase of melody, composer or source, date of writing or first appearance in print, alternative names, and comment. Includes also a melodic index and index of first words of lines of hymns.

470. Bailey, Albert Edward. *The Gospel in Hymns; Backgrounds and Interpretations.* New York: Charles Scribner's Sons, 1950. 600 pp.

Gives historical background on 313 hymns found in one or more of ten English-language mainline Protestant hymnals published between 1918 and 1941. Includes bibliography and indexes.

CHRISTIAN EDUCATION

471. Cully, Kendig Brubaker, ed. *The Westminster Dictionary of Christian Education.* Philadelphia: The Westminster Press, 1963. 812 pp.

A comprehensive, ecumenically oriented work with short, concise, signed articles on both theory and practice; approximately 390 contributors; extensive bibliography, table of subject headings with specific references to the bibliography.

472. Little, Lawrence C. *Researches in Personality, Character and Religious Education; A Bibliography of American Doctoral Dissertations, 1885–1959.* Pittsburgh: University of Pittsburgh Press, 1962. 215 pp.

Lists 6,304 dissertations in alphabetical order by author with university and date indicated for each; detailed subject index provided.

473. Little, Lawrence C. *Religion and Public Education: A*

Bibliography. 3d ed., rev. and enl. Pittsburgh: University of Pittsburgh Book Center, 1968. 214 pp.

Includes books and pamphlets by individuals and educational agencies, pronouncements and reports by religious bodies and public school systems, doctoral dissertations and master's theses, journal articles, and selected U.S. Supreme Court cases.

PASTORAL PSYCHOLOGY

474. Meissner, W. W. *Annotated Bibliography in Religion and Psychology.* New York: Academy of Religion and Mental Health, 1961. 235 pp.

Lists, annotates, and arranges in classified order 2,905 journal articles and books from both the scientific and the theological disciplines. Author index included.

475. Menges, Robert J., and Dittes, James E. *Psychological Studies of Clergymen: Abstracts of Research.* New York: Thomas Nelson & Sons, 1965. 202 pp.

Contains approximately 700 entries, annotated and classified, including books, journal articles, pamphlets, reports, etc., 75 percent of which are dated between 1955 and 1965. Includes index of authors, of instruments and methods, of samples and of topics.

MISSIONS

LIBRARY CATALOGS

476. New York (City). Missionary Research Library. *Dictionary Catalog of the Missionary Research Library, New York.* Boston: G. K. Hall & Co., 1968. 17 vols.

The catalog of one of the outstanding Protestant foreign missionary collections. Located since 1929 at Union Theological Seminary in New York; consists of more than 100,000 cataloged items, including books, periodicals, reports, and archival materials. The catalog contains author, title, and subject entries.

477. The Amistad Research Center. Fisk University, Nashville, Tenn. *Author and Added Entry Catalog of the American*

Missionary Association Archives; with references to schools and mission stations. Introduction by Clifton H. Johnson. Westport, Conn.: Greenwood Publishing Corp., 1970. 3 vols.

The outstanding archival collection for the study of the abolition movement, the education of Negroes in the South, and other "home" missionary activities 1846–1882. The collection consists of over 105,000 items, mostly letters, documenting the evangelistic and reform activities of the American Missionary Association. All the items in the catalog have been microfilmed and are available in this form in selected research libraries.

BIBLIOGRAPHY

478. Streit, Robert. *Bibliotheca Missionum.* Freiburg: Herder, 1916–1974. 29 vols. in 31. (Veröffentlichen des Internationalen Instituts für Missionswissenschaftliche Forschung.)

Monumental scholarly bibliography of Catholic missions, often cited as "Streit-Dindinger," since Johannes Dindinger continued the work begun by Robert Streit. Volumes are arranged by country or area, chronologically by year within a country or area, and by author within a given year. Provides full bibliographical detail, critical annotations, references to sources and locations in European libraries. Includes materials from the sixteenth century to the present. Indexes of authors, of persons, of subjects, and of places included in each volume.

479. Vriens, Livinius. *Critical Bibliography of Missiology.* Translated from the Dutch Ms. by Deodatus Tummers. Nijmegen: Bestelcentrale der V.S.K.B. (Dutch Association of Seminary and Monastery Librarians), 1960. 198 pp. (Bibliographia ad Usum Seminariorum, Vol. E2.)

Classified, annotated listing of Catholic works on mission theory, law, methodology, history, propaganda, and missiography. Index of authors and anonymous works included.

480. *Bibliografia Missionaria.* Comp. by Giovanni Rommerskirchen (and others). Rome, 1935 to date. Annual.

Publisher varies. Vol. 1 covers Jan. 1, 1933 to June 30, 1934. Contains classified arrangement of Catholic mission literature, although some Protestant works are also included. Provides

annual author and subject indexes and four-year cumulated
indexes.

481. Sinclair, John H., ed. *Protestantism in Latin America: A
Bibliographical Guide,* an annotated bibliography of selected
references mainly in English, Spanish and Portuguese and useful
bibliographical aids to assist the student and researcher in the
general field of Latin American studies. South Pasadena, Calif.:
William Carey Library, 1976. 414 pp.

Part One is a reprint of the 1967 edition and Part Two is the
new material of the 1976 edition. Together both parts list 3,115
works. Classified arrangement with author index. Comprehensive, scholarly work.

DICTIONARY, HANDBOOK, ENCYCLOPEDIA

482. Neill, Stephen; Anderson, Gerald; and Goodwin, John.
Concise Dictionary of the Christian World Mission. Nashville
and New York: Abingdon Press, 1971. 682 pp.

Brief, authoritative articles, most with bibliography, by over
two hundred specialists; covers five centuries of missionary en-
deavor; has cross-references; ecumenical and international in
perspective.

483. *Mission Handbook: North American Protestant Minis-
tries Overseas.* 11th ed. Monrovia, Calif.: Missions Advanced
Research and Communication Center (MARC), 1976. 589 pp.
1st ed., 1953.

Gives brief statistical information about church-related and
independent mission agencies. Also includes brief essays by specialists on current issues, lists of schools and professors of missions, and indexes.

484. *The Encyclopedia of Modern Christian Missions: The
Agencies.* Burton L. Goddard, ed. Camden, N.J.: Thomas Nelson & Sons, 1967. 743 pp.

Contains brief articles with historical and directory information on existing Protestant mission agencies throughout the
world. A publication of the faculty of Gordon Divinity School
(now Gordon-Conwell Theological Seminary).

SURVEY

485. Latourette, Kenneth Scott. *A History of the Expansion of Christianity.* New York: Harper & Brothers, 1937–1945. 7 vols.

A comprehensive, scholarly work surveying the growth of Christianity worldwide from the first through the twentieth century. Extensive bibliography with brief critical annotations in each volume.

ATLAS

486. Freitag, Anton (and others). *The Twentieth Century Atlas of the Christian World;* the expansion of Christianity through the centuries. New York: Hawthorn Books, Inc., 1963. 200 pp.

Translated from the French edition of 1959. Traces expansion of Christianity from a Catholic perspective. Numerous photographs and colored maps accompany the text. Index to text, illustrations, and notes on the illustrations provided.

ECUMENICS

LIBRARY CATALOG

487. World Council of Churches. Library. *Classified Catalog of the Ecumenical Movement, World Council of Churches, Geneva, Switzerland.* Boston: G. K. Hall & Co., 1972. 2 vols.

A classified catalog of "the most complete collection of literature on the ecumenical movement in the 20th century" (Introduction). Includes the schedule of the World Council of Churches classification system and an alphabetical index of names of individual authors and editors.

BIBLIOGRAPHY

488. Crow, Paul A., Jr. *The Ecumenical Movement in Bibliographical Outline.* New York: Department of Faith and Order, National Council of the Churches of Christ in the U.S.A., 1965. 80 pp.

Classified arrangement, unannotated. Includes chapters on bibliographies, reference works, periodicals, surveys, introductions, modern conciliar movements, church unions and union schemes, denominational ecumenism, biographies, and evangelical critics. Lists mostly English-language works; few Vatican II materials. Updates and supplements the two earlier works listed below.

489. Brandreth, Henry R. T. *Unity and Religion, A Bibliography.* London: A. & C. Black, Ltd., 1945. 159 pp.

A classified, annotated survey of both the primary and the secondary literature of reunion since the beginning of the nineteenth century. "Limited to those works which deal, more or less directly, with the visible unity and reunion of divided Christendom; movements which aim solely at co-operation between different Christian communions on social, economic or other matters of that nature, valuable as such movements may be, lie outside the scope of our inquiry" (Preface). Intended for English-language readers. Lists almost 1,200 items. Includes index of authors and a brief subject index.

490. Senaud, Auguste. *Christian Unity, A Bibliography;* selected titles concerning international relations between churches and international Christian movements. Geneva: World's Committee of Y.M.C.A.'s, 1937. 173 pp.

A classified and chronological unannotated listing of almost 2,000 books and articles from the middle of the nineteenth century onward dealing with both the "Faith and Order" and the "Life and Work" aspects of the ecumenical movement. Includes both churches and international Christian movements in its scope. Author-subject index provided.

491. Lescrauwaet, J. F. *Critical Bibliography of Ecumenical Literature.* Nijmegen: Bestel Centrale, 1965. 93 pp. (Bibliographia ad Usum Seminariorum, Vol. 7.)

An annotated, classified bibliography from a post-Vatican II Catholic perspective. Section I deals with the history, doctrine, and practice of the various churches in the ecumenical movement; Section II deals with the ecumenical movement itself. Lists 351 works; index of authors and anonymous works.

492. *Internationale oekumenische Bibliographie. International Ecumenical Bibliography. Bibliographie Oecuménique Internationale. Bibliografía Ecuménica Internacional. (IOB)* 1962/63 to date. Munich: Chr. Kaiser; Mainz: Matthias-Grünewald, 1967 to date. Annual.

A comprehensive, classified, international, interconfessional bibliography of ecumenical literature, including journal articles, books, reports; some brief annotations. Publication date runs about six years behind the date of the material indexed. Consists of two main sections: The Churches, and The Theological Questions. Provides indexes of authors, of reviews, of periodical volumes examined, and of subjects.

SURVEY

493. Rouse, Ruth, and Neill, Stephen Charles, eds. *A History of the Ecumenical Movement.* London: S.P.C.K.; Philadelphia: The Westminster Press, 1967–1970. 2 vols.

Vol. 1, 1517–1948, first published 1954; 2d ed. with revised bibliography, 1967. Vol. 2, 1948–1968, ed. by Harold E. Fey, 1970.

The authoritative work on the ecumenical movement, written by Protestant and Orthodox scholars and church leaders. Extensive bibliographies and indexes in both volumes.

SOURCES

494. Bell, George Kennedy Allen. *Documents of Christian Unity.* London and New York: Oxford University Press, 1924–1958. 4 vols.

1st series, 1920–1924 (1924); 2d series, 1924–1930 (1930); 3d series, 1930–1948 (1948); 4th series, 1948–1957 (1958).

Contains the important ecumenical documents and plans of union from throughout the world.

COMPARATIVE RELIGION

BIBLIOGRAPHY

495. Adams, Charles J., ed. *A Reader's Guide to the Great Religions.* 2d ed. New York: Free Press, 1977. 521 pp.
1st ed., 1965.
Long, bibliographic essays by specialists on the world's major religions. An especially useful tool for the nonspecialist who is teaching a survey course in college, university, or parish.

496. Berkowitz, Morris I., and Johnson, J. Edmund. *Social Scientific Studies of Religion: A Bibliography.* Pittsburgh: University of Pittsburgh Press, 1967. 258 pp.
Lists both books and journal articles on the history and development of various religions, as well as the relation of religion to other social institutions and behavior, to education and communication, to social issues and social changes. Broad scope, detailed classification scheme, and complete author index.

497. *International Bibliography of the History of Religions. Bibliographie Internationale de l'Histoire des Religions.* . . . 1952 to date. Leiden: E. J. Brill, 1954 to date. Annual.
Classified arrangement with author indexes beginning in the 1958/59 issue. Published by the International Association for the History of Religion with financial support from UNESCO. Includes books and periodical articles. There is a time lag of two to four years between the date of publication of the annual issue of *IBHR* and the date of the materials listed.

DICTIONARIES

498. *A Dictionary of Comparative Religion.* S. G. F. Brandon, gen. ed. London: Weidenfeld & Nicolson, Ltd.; New York: Charles Scribner's Sons, 1970. 704 pp.
Short, signed articles by British scholars, with bibliographies. Includes synoptic index listing all articles related to each of fifteen major religions, and general index. Useful ready-reference tool.

499. Parrinder, Edward Geoffrey. *A Dictionary of Non-Christian Religions.* Philadelphia: The Westminster Press, 1973. 320 pp.

1st British ed., 1971.

Gives special attention to Hinduism, Buddhism, and Islam, but includes other religions, ancient and modern, with the exception of Christianity and the Bible. Brief definitions without bibliography. Short bibliography appended. Numerous photographs and drawings.

See also *Encyclopaedia of Religion and Ethics* (no. 96).

PRIMITIVE RELIGIONS, MYTHOLOGY, FOLKLORE

500. Gray, Louis Herbert, ed. *The Mythology of All Races.* Boston: Marshall Jones, 1916–1932. 13 vols.

The most complete work on the subject in English. The general index makes it a useful reference tool.

501. Grimal, Pierre, ed. *Larousse World Mythology.* Tr. by Patricia Beardsworth. New York: G. P. Putnam's Sons. 1965. 560 pp.

A useful one-volume reference tool.

502. Jobes, Gertrude. *Dictionary of Mythology, Folklore and Symbols.* New York: Scarecrow Press, 1961–1963. 3 vols.

Comprehensive dictionary giving brief definitions as well as historical and interpretative background. Vol. 3 contains index with table of deities, heroes, and personalities and table of mythological applications (supernatural forms, realms, things).

HINDUISM

503. Walker, Benjamin. *The Hindu World;* an encyclopedic survey of Hinduism. New York and Washington: Frederick A. Praeger, Inc., 1968. 2 vols.

A comprehensive work based on "the standard works of recognized authorities, supplemented by material drawn from traditional Indian sources" (Preface). Alphabetical arrangement with detailed subject index and many cross-references. Bibliography appended to most articles.

504. Dowson, John. *A Classical Dictionary of Hindu Mythology and Religion, Geography, History, and Literature.* 11th ed. London: Routledge & Kegan Paul, Ltd., 1968. 411 pp.

1st ed., 1879.

11th ed. not greatly changed. Old, but still useful.

BUDDHISM

505. Humphreys, Christmas. *A Popular Dictionary of Buddhism.* London: Arco Publications, Ltd., 1962. 223 pp.

Intended for the English-speaking student who is more than a casual reader, but not a trained scholar. Brief definitions.

506. *Encyclopaedia of Buddhism.* Ed. by G. P. Malalasekera. Colombo: Published by the Government of Ceylon, 1961 ff.

Vols. 1–2 and part of Vol. 3 (A–Budal) have been published thus far. A scientific, scholarly work.

ISLAM

507. *The Encyclopaedia of Islam,* new edition . . . ed. by H. A. R. Gibb, J. H. Kramers, E. Lévi-Provençal, J. Schacht . . . under the patronage of the International Union of Academies. Leiden: E. J. Brill; London: Luzac, 1954 ff.

1st ed., 1911–1938, 4 vols. and supplement.

Thus far Vols. 1–3 and part of Vol. 4 have been published (A-Karimi) in this new edition.

A detailed, scholarly work with signed articles and bibliographies. Until the new edition is completed, the 1st edition must be consulted.

508. *Shorter Encyclopaedia of Islam.* H. A. R. Gibb and J. H. Kramers, eds. Ithaca, N.Y.: Cornell University Press, 1953. 671 pp.

Includes all the articles from the 1st edition of the *Encyclopaedia of Islam* (no. 507) that relate to religion and law, with some revisions; also includes a few new articles and an updated bibliography.

CHAPTER IX

Biography; Almanacs, Directories, and Yearbooks; Quotation and Poetry Indexes; Style Manuals

BIOGRAPHY

Biographical reference works can be divided into three types: international, national or regional, and occupational. And these three types can be subdivided into works treating persons now living (current biography) or persons now dead (retrospective biography). Not all current biographical works are equally reliable, as some are commercial or "vanity" enterprises in which the biographee must subscribe to the work or pay a fee to have his/her name included. Listed here are but a few of the more basic, standard, reliable works for international, United States, British, and occupational biography. See also nos. 328, 329, 381, 411, 412, 413, 421, 435, 439, 445 for additional biographical works. Also, many of the encyclopedias and dictionaries listed throughout this work contain biographical information, as indicated.

INDEXES TO BIOGRAPHIES

These are works that list places where biographical information may be found concerning a particular person but do not give the biographical information itself.

509. Arnim, Max. *Internationale Personalbibliographie, 1800–1943.* 2 verb. u. stark verm. Aufl. Stuttgart: Anton Hiersemann, 1952. 2 vols.

——. Bd. III, 1944–1959 and Nachträge, von Gerhard Bock und Franz Hodes. Stuttgart: Hiersemann, 1961–1963. 659 pp.

An index to bibliographies of individuals. Such bibliographies often contain biographies also.

510. *Biography Index;* a cumulative index to biographical materials in books and magazines. New York: The H. W. Wilson Company, 1946 to date. Quarterly with annual and three-year cumulations.

An index to any biographical material contained in over 1,700 journals as well as in current books. Includes persons both living and dead. Main section, arranged alphabetically by name of biographee, is followed by section listing biographees alphabetically by occupation or profession.

511. Hyamson, Albert Montefiore. *A Dictionary of Universal Biography of All Ages and of All Peoples.* 2d ed., entirely rewritten. New York: E. P. Dutton & Co., Inc., 1951. 697 pp.

An index to persons listed in 24 standard biographical works.

512. The New York Times. *The New York Times Obituaries Index 1858–1968.* New York: The New York Times, 1970. 1,136 pp.

Lists all the names that appeared under "Deaths" in *The New York Times* for 110 years. Indicates year, date, section (if any), page, and column of the original news story. Microfilm of *The New York Times* is available in many libraries.

INTERNATIONAL

513. *Webster's Biographical Dictionary;* a dictionary of names of noteworthy persons, with pronunciations and concise biographies. Springfield, Mass.: G. & C. Merriam Company, 1976. 1,697 pp.

Contains brief biographical information on upward of 40,000 people, living and dead. Emphasis on American and British persons. A basic one-volume biographical tool.

514. *Current Biography.* 1940 to date. New York: The H. W. Wilson Company, 1940 to date. Monthly with annual cumulation.

Annual cumulation is entitled *Current Biography Yearbook.* It provides index for the current year as well as for the previous ten years. Contains 300–500 biographies annually, with portraits and references for further reading.

515. *The International Who's Who.* 1935 to date. London:

Europa Publications, Ltd.; George Allen & Unwin, Ltd., 1935 to date. Annual, although somewhat irregular.

Gives short biographies of notable persons throughout the world.

516. *Who's Who in the World.* 1971/72 to date. Chicago: Marquis Who's Who, Inc., 1971 to date.

Published about every three years by the company that has published *Who's Who in America* for over 75 years. Lists "those individuals who are of current reference interest and inquiry throughout the world, the movers and shakers of our civilization—the people about whom other people ask questions" (Preface).

UNITED STATES

517. *Who's Who in America,* a biographical dictionary of notable living men and women. Chicago: Marquis Who's Who, Inc., 1899 to date. Biennial.

The standard current biographical reference work for the United States. The 38th ed. (1974/75) contains over 73,000 biographical entries. It also has a section listing names of the 74,000 biographees in the Marquis regional library composed of *Who's Who in the East, Who's Who in the Midwest, Who's Who in the South and Southwest,* and *Who's Who in the West.* Includes biographical sketch, home address, and bibliography of works written by the biographee.

518. *Who Was Who in America: Historical Volume, 1607–1896;* a component volume of Who's Who in American History. Chicago: Marquis Who's Who, Inc., 1963. 670 pp.

Provides biographical sketches for the period up to the beginning of Vol. 1 of *Who Was Who in America,* 1897. See no. 519.

519. *Who Was Who in America;* a companion biographical reference work to Who's Who in America. Chicago: Marquis Who's Who, Inc., 1942–1968. 4 vols.

Contents: Vol. 1, 1897–1942; Vol. 2, 1943–1950; Vol. 3, 1951–1960; Vol. 4, 1961–1968. These, together with no. 518, make up a series entitled Who's Who in American History.

Includes sketches that have appeared in *Who's Who in America* (no. 517) but have been removed because of death. Vol. 4

contains an index to Vols. 1–4 and to the Historical Volume (no. 518).

520. *Dictionary of American Biography;* under the auspices of the American Council of Learned Societies. New York: Charles Scribner's Sons, 1928–1937. 20 vols. and index.

————. Supplements 1–4. New York: Charles Scribner's Sons, 1944–1974.

The standard scholarly American biographical work comparable to the British *Dictionary of National Biography* (no. 525). Contains articles of considerable length with bibliographies. Does not include minor names or living persons. Arranged alphabetically.

521. *The National Cyclopaedia of American Biography.* New York: James T. White & Co., Inc., 1892–1977. Vols. 1–57. (In progress.) Some volumes issued in revised edition.

A more comprehensive work than the *Dictionary of American Biography* (no. 520). Unsigned articles, no bibliography. Use of index is essential as arrangement in each volume is not alphabetical by biographee, but according to the vocation or career of the biographee.

————. *Current volumes,* A-L. New York: James T. White & Co., Inc., 1930–1972. (In progress.)

Includes living persons only. "After the death of a subject published in a Current Series volume, his biography is reprinted in final form in a Permanent Series volume" (Preface, Current Series Vol. L). Volume letters in the Current Series indicate sequence only, and bear no relation to the names of persons included in the contents. Vol. K supplements the previous volumes in the Current Series.

————. *Index,* Permanent Series (numbered volumes) and Current Series (lettered volumes). Clifton, N.J.: James T. White & Co., Inc., 1975. 546 pp.

Great Britain

522. *Who's Who,* an annual biographical dictionary. London: A. & C. Black Ltd., 1849 to date. Annual.

Until 1897 this work listed only titled and official classes. After that it listed prominent people in many fields. Primarily

British in scope. Gives brief biographical sketch, address, and works written.

523. *Who Was Who;* a companion to Who's Who, containing the biographies of those who died during the period. London: A. & C. Black, Ltd., 1929–1961. 5 vols.

Contents: Vol. 1, 1897–1915; Vol. 2, 1916–1928; Vol. 3, 1929–1940; Vol. 4, 1941–1950; Vol. 5, 1951–1960.

524. *Who's Who in History.* Vols. 1–4, Oxford: Basil Blackwell & Mott, Ltd., 1960–1973; Vol. 5, New York: Harper & Row, Publishers, Inc., 1975.

Contents: Vol. 1, British Isles, 55 B.C.–A.D. 1485, by W. O. Hassal (1960); Vol. 2, England, 1485–1603, by C. R. N. Routh (1961); Vol. 3, England, 1603–1714, by C. P. Hill (1965); Vol. 4, England, 1714–1789, by G. Treasure (1973); Vol. 5, England, 1789–1837, by G. Treasure (1975).

Written for the general reader. Each volume contains 200–300 biographies, arranged chronologically by date of death.

525. *Dictionary of National Biography.* Ed. by Sir Leslie Stephen and Sir Sidney Lee. (Reissue.) London: Smith, Elder and Co., 1908–1909. 22 vols. (Reprinted 1938.)

Vols. 1–21 first published 1885–1901.

Contents: Vols. 1–21, A-Z; Vol. 22, 1st supplement, Additional names, 1901.

————. 2d–7th supplements. Oxford: University Press, 1912–1971. 6 vols.

————. Index and epitome, ed. by Sir Sidney Lee. London: Smith, Elder and Co., 1903–1913. 2 vols.

The standard scholarly British biographical work; includes notable persons from the British Isles and the colonies, including Americans of the Colonial period. Excludes living persons. Longer articles for more important persons. Articles are signed and include bibliographies. The supplements cover the period to 1950.

526. *Dictionary of National Biography. The Concise Dictionary.* Oxford: University Press, 1903. (Reprinted 1953–1961.) 2 vols.

The reprint with revisions covers the period to 1950, with abstracts of the articles in the larger work (no. 525). Also serves as an index to the larger work.

OCCUPATIONAL

527. *Who's Who in Religion.* 2d ed. Chicago: Marquis Who's Who, Inc., 1977. 736 pp.

Brief biographical sketches of more than 18,000 American clergy, church officials, religious educators, and lay leaders.

528. *Contemporary Authors;* a bio-bibliographical guide to current authors and their works. James M. Ethridge, ed. Detroit: Gale Research Co., 1962 to date. Semiannual with cumulated index every two years.

Gives up-to-date biographical information on authors from many countries in the humanities, social sciences, and sciences.

529. *Directory of American Scholars.* 6th ed. Ed. by the Jaques Cattell Press. New York and London: R. R. Bowker Company, 1974. 4 vols.

Contents: Vol. 1, History; Vol. 2, English, Speech, and Drama; Vol. 3, Foreign Languages, Linguistics, and Philology; Vol. 4, Philosophy, Religion, and Law.

Provides brief biographical information, including bibliography, for each entry.

ALMANACS, DIRECTORIES, AND YEARBOOKS

Listed here are some of the more useful reference works providing quick access to a wide variety of facts, statistics, names, addresses, etc.

GENERAL

530. *The World Almanac and Book of Facts.* New York and Cleveland: Newspaper Enterprise Association, Inc., 1868 to date. Annual.

One of the most useful, comprehensive, and reliable of the single-volume compendiums of both historical and current information. Contains a general index in the front of the volume.

ASSOCIATIONS

531. *Encyclopedia of Associations.* Detroit: Gale Research Co., 1956 to date. Biennial.

Contents: Vol. 1, National organizations of the United States; Vol. 2, Geographic index and executive index; Vol. 3, New associations.

The first place to turn when looking for directory information concerning any organization in the United States.

FOUNDATIONS AND GRANT SUPPORT

532. *The Foundation Directory.* 6th ed. Prep. by the Foundation Center. New York: Distr. by Columbia University Press, 1977. 661 pp.

1st ed., 1960.

The basic work for information on over 6,000 foundations. Arranged geographically by state, alphabetically within each state. Indexes of field of interest; of donors, trustees, and administrators; and of foundations.

533. *Annual Register of Grant Support,* 1969 to date. Chicago: Marquis Who's Who, Inc., Academic Media, 1969 to date. Annual.

Provides information on nonrepayable financial support from "government agencies, public and private foundations, business and industrial firms, unions, educational and professional associations, and special interest organizations" (Introduction). Classified arrangement, alphabetical within subject classes. Includes subject, organization and program, geographic, and personnel indexes.

EDUCATION

534. *The World of Learning, 1975–76.* 26th ed. London: Europa Publications, Ltd., 1975. 2 vols.

Contents: Vol. 1, A-P; Vol. 2, Q-Z.

Arranged alphabetically by country. Gives information on national academies and institutes, learned societies, libraries, museums, art galleries, universities and colleges throughout the world. Contains an index of institutions.

535. *The National Faculty Directory, 1977.* 7th ed. Detroit: Gale Research Co., 1977. 2 vols.

"An alphabetical list with addresses, of about 449,000 members of teaching faculties at junior colleges, colleges and universities in the United States and at selected Canadian institutions."

536. *American Universities and Colleges.* 11th ed. W. Todd Furniss, ed. Washington: American Council on Education, 1973. 1,879 pp.

Gives detailed information on faculty, administration, degree program, enrollment, requirements, costs, etc., for colleges and universities in the United States. Arranged geographically by states and alphabetically by institution's name within states. Contains numerous statistical tables as well as institutional index and general index.

UNITED STATES

537. U.S. Bureau of the Census. *Statistical Abstract of the United States.* 1878 to date. Washington: Government Printing Office, 1879 to date. Annual.

"The standard summary of statistics on the social, political, and economic organization of the United States. It is designed to serve as a convenient volume for statistical reference and as a guide to other statistical publications and sources" (Preface). Often includes statistics for the last ten or fifteen years as well as current statistics, although some data go back to 1790.

INTERNATIONAL

538. *The Statesman's Year-book;* statistical and historical annual of the states of the world, 1864 to date. London: Macmillan Publishers, Ltd.; New York: St. Martin's Press, 1864 to date.

Provides up-to-date statistics and other information on international organizations, Great Britain and the Commonwealth, the United States and each of its fifty states, and all the other countries of the world. Bibliography provided for each country and state. Index included. A reliable and extremely useful work.

UNITED NATIONS

539. United Nations. *Yearbook of the United Nations,* 1946/47 to date. New York: United Nations, Department of Public Information, 1947 to date. Annual.

"Comprehensive, succinct account . . . of the very many discussions, decisions and activities of the United Nations and the inter-governmental organizations related to it" (Foreword). Also contains bibliography, subject index, and index of names.

QUOTATION AND POETRY INDEXES

These works, and many others similar to them, are most useful for locating the source and exact form of a quotation from prose or poetry that one wants to use in a sermon.

540. Bartlett, John. *Familiar Quotations;* a collection of passages, phrases and proverbs traced to their sources in ancient and modern literature. 14th ed., rev. and enl., Emily Morison Beck, ed. Boston and Toronto: Little, Brown and Company, 1968. 1,750 pp.

1st ed., 1855.

A veritable mine for preacher or public speaker; worth reading for its own sake as well as for the stimulation it provides to read more of the authors quoted. Arranged in chronological order by author. Contains also memorable quotations from the Bible and the Book of Common Prayer. Extensive key-word index with over 117,000 entries.

541. Granger, Edith. *Granger's Index to Poetry.* 6th ed., completely rev. and enl., indexing anthologies publ. through Dec. 31, 1970. Ed. by William James Smith. New York: Columbia University Press, 1973. 2,223 pp.

1st ed., 1904.

Provides access to poems by title and first line index, author index, and subject index. The title and first line index directs the user to one or more of 514 poetry anthologies where the particular poem may be found.

STYLE MANUALS

542. Chicago. University Press. *A Manual of Style;* for authors, editors, and copywriters. 12th ed., rev. Chicago and London: The University of Chicago Press, 1969. 546 pp.

Often cited as the *Chicago Manual of Style,* this work is a detailed, authoritative, well-illustrated manual on forms and style for footnotes, bibliographies, punctuation, abbreviations, quotations, etc., to guide writers, editors, typographers, and others. Includes subject index, glossary of technical terms, and bibliography.

543. Turabian, Kate L. *A Manual for Writers of Term Papers, Theses and Dissertations.* 4th ed. Chicago and London: The University of Chicago Press, 1973. 216 pp.

Adapts the instructions of the Chicago *Manual of Style* (no. 542) to the producing of a typewritten script. A basic, authoritative guide, well arranged, illustrated, and indexed. As styles change, usually toward simplification, only the latest edition should be used of this or any other manual of style.

Author
and Title Index

References are to entry numbers.

Abbot, E. "The Literature of the Doctrine of a Future Life," 306

Abingdon Bible Commentary, The, F. C. Eiselen, E. Lewis, and D. G. Downey, 208

Abingdon Bible Handbook, E. P. Blair, 217

Ackroyd, P. R. *Bible Bibliography, 1967–1973; Old Testament,* 227

Adams, C. J. *A Reader's Guide to the Great Religions,* 495

Addis, W. E., and Arnold, T. *A Catholic Dictionary,* 405

Aharoni, Y., and Avi-Yonah, M. *The Macmillan Bible Atlas,* 221

Ahlstrom, S. E. *A Religious History of the American People,* 373

————. *Theology in America: The Major Protestant Voices from Puritanism to Neo-Orthodoxy,* 372

Aids to a Theological Library, American Theological Library Association, 39

Aids to a Theological Library, J. B. Trotti, 40

Aland, K.; Black, M.; Martini, C. M.; Metzger, B. M.; and Wikgren, A. *The Greek New Testament,* 262

————; Nestle, Eberhard; and Nestle, Erwin. *Novum Testamentum Graece,* 261

Albright, W. F., and Freedman, D. N. *The Anchor Bible,* 195

Aldrich, E. V., and Camp, T. E. *Using Theological Books and Libraries,* 9

Allmen, J.-J. von. *A Companion to the Bible,* 153

Alphabetical Arrangement of Main Entries from the Shelf List, Union Theological Seminary, New York, 28

Alphabetical Subject Index and Index Encyclopaedia to Periodical Articles on Religion, 1890–1899, An, E. C. Richardson, 47

America: History and Life, 367

American Baptist Seminary of the West, Covina Campus. *The Tools of Biblical Interpretation; A Bibliographical Guide,* 128

Archiv für Reformationsgeschichte. Beiheft. Literaturbericht, 344

Archive for Reformation History. Supplement. Literature Review, 344

Armstrong, M. W.; Loetscher, L. A.; and Anderson, C. A. *The Presbyterian Enterprise,* 447

Arnim, M. *Internationale Personalbibliographie, 1800–1943,* 509

Arnold, T., and Addis, W. E. *A Catholic Dictionary,* 405

Arnold, W.; Eysenck, H. J.; and Meili, R. *Encyclopedia of Psychology,* 110

As Modern Writers See Jesus, A. T. Case, 300

Atiya, A. S. *The Crusade: Historiography and Bibliography,* 338

Atlas of Israel, 223

Atlas of the Bible, L. H. Grollenberg, 218

Atlas of the Biblical World, D. Baly and A. D. Tushingham, 224

Attwater, D. *A Catholic Dictionary* (The Catholic Encyclopaedic Dictionary), 406

Authentic New Testament, The, Hugh J. Schonfield, 272

Author and Added Entry Catalog of the American Missionary Association Archives, The Amistad Research Center, 477

Author Catalog of Disciples of Christ and Related Religious Groups, An, C. E. Spencer, 422

Authorized Version, 160

Avi-Yonah, M., and Aharoni, Y. *The Macmillan Bible Atlas,* 221

Ayer Directory of Publications, 66

Ayer, J. C. *A Source Book for Ancient Church History,* 334

Ayres, S. G. *Jesus Christ Our Lord,* 299

Bailey, A. E. *The Gospel in Hymns; Backgrounds and Interpretations,* 470

Bainton, R. H., and Gritsch, E. W. *Bibliography of the Continental Reformation,* 341

Baker's Dictionary of Christian Ethics, 309

Baker's Dictionary of Theology, 289

Baldwin, M. W. *Christianity Through the Thirteenth Century,* 340

Baly, D., and Tushingham, A. D. *Atlas of the Biblical World,* 224

Baptist Bibliography, A, E. C. Starr, 414

Barber, C. J. *The Minister's Library,* 6

Barclay, W. *The Daily Study Bible,* 284

———. *The New Testament, A New Translation,* 275

Bardenhewer, O. *Patrology; The Lives and Works of the Fathers of the Church,* 323

Barrow, J. G. *A Bibliography of Bibliographies in Religion,* 21

Bartlett, J. *Familiar Quotations,* 540

————; Brown, R. E.; and Murphy, R. E. *The Jerome Biblical Commentary,* 213

Formation of the United Church of Christ (U.S.A.), The, H. P. Keiling, 450

Foundation Directory, The, 532

Freedman, D. N., and Albright, W. F. *The Anchor Bible,* 195

Freidel, F. B., and Showman, R. K. *Harvard Guide to American History,* 364

Freitag, A. *The Twentieth Century Atlas of the Christian World,* 486

Fritsch, C. T.; Brock, S. P.; and Jellicoe, S. *A Classified Bibliography of the Septuagint,* 237

Fuller, R. C.; Johnston, L.; and Kearns, C. *A New Catholic Commentary on Holy Scripture,* 214

Funk & Wagnalls Modern Guide to Synonyms and Related Words, S. I. Hayakawa, 123

Gant, W. J. *The Moffatt Bible Concordance,* 188

Gaustad, E. S. *Historical Atlas of Religion in America,* 382

Geden, A. S., and Moulton, W. F. *A Concordance to the Greek Testament,* 267

Gee, H., and Hardy, W. J. *Documents Illustrative of English Church History,* 362

Gehman, H. S. *The New Westminster Dictionary of the Bible,* 150

General Catalogue of Printed Books, British Museum, 34

German "Books in Print": *Verzeichnis lieferbarer Bücher,* 80

Gesenius, H. F. W. *Gesenius' Hebrew Grammar,* 230

Gill, A. *A Bibliography of Baptist Writings on Baptism, 1900–1968,* 415

Glanzman, G. S., and Fitzmyer, J. A. *An Introductory Bibliography for the Study of the Scripture,* 129

Good News Bible, 179

Goodspeed, E. J., and Smith, J. M. P. *The Complete Bible; An American Translation,* 173

Goodwin, J.; Neill, S. C.; and Anderson, G. *Concise Dictionary of the Christian World Mission,* 482|

Gore, C.; Goudge, H. L.; and Guillaume, A. *A New Commentary on Holy Scripture,* 207

Gospel in Hymns, The; Backgrounds and Interpretations, A. E. Bailey, 470

Goudge, H. L.; Gore, C.; and Guillaume, A. *A New Commentary on Holy Scripture,* 207

Government Publications and Their Use, L. F. Schmeckebier and R. B. Eastin, 94